Korean Historical Dramas

Heroes and Villains in Korean History

by Mi Park

CHP

Coal Harbour Publishing

Korean Historical Dramas. Heroes and Villains in Korean History

Publication Data

———————

Author: Park, Mi
Title: Korean Historical Dramas. Heroes and Villains in Korean History /Park, Mi--1st ed.
Publication date: October 2019
Publisher: Coal Harbour Publishing Ltd.

ISBN 978-1-989043-42-4 (E-book)
ISBN 978-1-989043-41-7 (Paperback)
CHP

Table of Contents

Romanization of Korean Words

This book uses the Revised Romanization of Korean (RRK) system instead of the McCune–Reischauer system or other methods. A notable feature of the RRK is the spelling of some Korean letters (ㄱ, ㄷ, ㅂ, and ㅈ). For instance, the Korean letter "ㄱ" is spelled "g" instead of "k", as in Goguryeo (고구려) as opposed to Koguryeo. Similarly, the Korean letter "ㄷ" is written as "d" as opposed to "t", as in Donghak (동학) instead of Tonghak. The letters below indicate examples of different English spellings of some Korean letters.

ㄱ → g (k)   ㄷ → b (p)   ㅈ → j (ch)   ㄷ → d (t)

Table 1. Examples of Differently Romanized Korean Words

Korean Words	RRK system	Other spelling
신라	Silla	Shilla
발해	Balhae	Parhae
가야	Gaya (Kaya)	Kaya
고구려	Goguryeo	Koguryeo
백제	Baekje	Paekje
고조선	Gojoseon	Gochosun
조선	Joseon	Chosun
고종	Gojong	Kojong
동학	Donghak	Tonghak
광주	Gwangju	Kwangju
대구	Daegu	Taegu
기생	Giesaeng	Kisaeng
제주도	Jejudo	Chejudo

Introduction

Korean Historical Drama (Sageuk)

Watching historical TV series and films is a highly entertaining way to be introduced to Korean history. In fact, "sageuk", referring to historical TV series dramas in Korean, may serve as an educational tool for understanding Korean culture and politics.

Historical dramas and movies can shape historical narratives as to how a nation's history is remembered. The memory of the past is essential to the existence of a nation. In this regard, they are an inseparable part of the making of a nation. The French philosopher and sociologist, Ernest Renan (1823-1892), has once stated that a nation is a soul in possession of common memories (Renan, 1882). To have a sense of national belonging, people must have some shared memories of a glorious past of their ancestors. As Renan put it,

> A heroic past, great men, glory (…), this is the social capital upon which one bases a national idea. To have common glories in the past and to have a common will in the present; to have performed great deeds together, to wish to perform still more, these are the essential conditions for being a people. (Renan, 1882)

As Renan's insightful statement suggests, one may find many Korean "sageuk" and historical films that highlight great historical achievements by Koreans in the past. For instance, the highly revered King Sejong is frequently featured in many films and TV dramas as the inventor of the Korean alphabet and the promoter of scientific developments.

Equally important to the national identity are the memories of common suffering. Sageuk and historical films may show the ways in which Koreans selectively recollect some historical events as the source of their suffering and national humiliation. As Renan points out,

> One loves in proportion to the sacrifices to which one has consented, and in proportion to the ills that one has suffered. (…) More valuable by far (…) is the fact of sharing, in the past, a glorious heritage and regrets, (…), or the fact of having suffered, enjoyed, and hoped together. (…), indeed, suffering in common unifies more than joy does. Where national memories are concerned, griefs are of more value than triumphs, for they impose duties, and require a common effort. A nation is therefore a large-scale solidarity, constituted by the feeling of the sacrifices that one has made in the past and of those that one is prepared to make in the future. (Renan, 1882)

True to Renan's observation, indeed, historical K-dramas are replete with stories of Korean people's suffering at the hands of corrupt power-holders or foreign invaders. At the same time, they provide inspiring stories about individual sacrifices and collective efforts to bring the culprits to justice. Historical dramas entailing heroic sacrifices may inspire the viewers with the sense of duty to make similar efforts for the collective good. In this regard, watching historical K-drama is akin to taking part in the making and the re-making of the Korean nation. They can also provide a useful lens through which people can gain a valuable insight into how a nation is being perceived as an "imagined community" of shared political values and ideals (Anderson, 1991).

Thanks to the widespread popularity of K-pop, more and more people take an interest in Korean culture and turn to Korean TV series dramas and movies as a quick and easy guide to understanding Korean society (Chung, A 2018). The problem is how to reconcile the gap between fiction and historical reality. Historical dramas almost always contain fictional stories and thus, they may lead to a distorted understanding of Korean history.

This book is conceived as an aid to navigate through a host of historical TV dramas and films on Korea. Separating real historical events from fiction, it provides a broad historical context in which relevant films and TV series deal with specific historical events, so that the viewers can keep a critical distance from highly dramatized and emotionally charged events in historical K-dramas. Albeit problems of historical distortion exist, historical dramas and cinematographic films can be a useful tool to unearth a national history.

How to Use this book

This book is structured in the following way. Each chapter begins with an overview of major political events and important historical figures pertinent to Korean kingdoms under the spotlight. The history section is accompanied by information boxes dealing with TV series and movies relevant to historical figures mentioned in the overview.

Sageuk usually consists of 16 to 24 episodes, with each episode running for about 1 hour. All historical dramas are based on the template of story telling that mixes real historical events with fictional love stories. While most historical dramas contain political plots and intrigues, some historical dramas entail many epic battle scenes or focus on a love triangle with historical events only as a backdrop. Although love stories are largely fictional, most dramas depict a fair number of historical events involving real historical figures.

The historical overview section focuses on four areas: inter-state relations (geopolitics), domestic power struggle in the royal court or government, popular discontent (social grievances), and culture (arts and science). The four areas are frequently used as major themes for dramatization in the manner that they accentuate the common suffering and the common glories of the Korean nation.

First, geopolitics or the relationship between states around the Korean peninsula matters a great deal since it greatly affects the rise and fall of states. Numerous Korean monarchs fell to foreign invasions, or while they were actively engaged in military campaigns for territorial expansion. When spared from total collapse, the weakened monarchy became a tributary state to more powerful neighboring countries. As many historical K-dramas will show, geopolitical rivalry is a popular theme for dramatization, or at least used as an essential backdrop of domestic power struggle in the royal court.

Secondly, the history overview section focuses on domestic power struggle among the ruling elite in the royal court. Plenty K-dramas deal with political intrigues involving the ruling house of the royal court and powerful aristocratic families. As many historical dramas demonstrate, earlier kingdoms on the Korean peninsula experienced a constant power struggle between the monarchs and powerful aristocratic families. While monarchical power in Korea had been often constrained by powerful aristocratic families, the political elite was often divided, as they fought over various issues including the succession to the throne or domestic policies over land reform and taxation. While watching K-dramas, the viewers can dig deeper by exploring the political reasons behind many of the court intrigues.

Third, the history overview covers, albeit limited, the life of ordinary Korean masses. It provides a glimpse of social stratification and sources of popular grievances. Coalescing with the first two elements (geopolitics and domestic power rivalry), political dissatisfaction of the commoners (peasants, artisans, merchants) and slaves had played a significant role in strengthening oppositional forces against the status quo in Korean history. Some K-dramas such as "Mung bean Flowers" delve into the issue of popular grievances that had an impact on domestic power rivalry in the royal court.

Lastly, this book highlights major cultural and scientific achievements made by Koreans. As Renan points out, a nation is a cultural and political community of people, remembering the glories of their ancestral past. While the source of national glories may vary, most nations largely celebrate cultural and scientific achievements as well as military victories against foreign invaders or own territorial expansion.

Throughout the book, the history overview section of each chapter aims to deal with salient figures and historical events in the four areas. All historical overview sections are interlaced with an overview of K-dramas relevant to significant historical events and figures under discussion. Before you start watching K-dramas, you may turn to chapters that deal with the historical background of the drama of your choice. For a complete list of selected films and TV series mentioned in the book, please see the appendix at the end of the book.

Most K-dramas are available on numerous online streaming sites. Some of the most popular sites include: Viki, Netflix, Dramacool, Viu, Kocowa, Dailymotion, among many others. Type your choice of historical drama on your computer. It should be noted that the most popular streaming platforms such as Netflix or Viki might not have older historical TV series that were released more than five years ago. In such a case, try other web-based platforms to find older episodes. While watching K-dramas, use your historical imagination empowered by the basic historical knowledge provided in this book. You will soon find yourself being inspired by K-dramas to learn more about the Korean people, their history and culture.

Chapter 1

Ancient Korean Kingdoms: From Gojoseon to Unified Silla

The Chronology of Korean Kingdoms

The first recorded Korean kingdom is Gojoseon that came into existence in 2333 BC. In the first century BC, Gojoseon disintegrated into several rivaling smaller states (e.g. Buyeo, Okjeo, and Nakrang) as the result of the invasions led by the Han Empire of China. Eventually, the three kingdoms, called Goguryeo, Silla, Baekje, emerged as the most powerful states on the Korean peninsula, as they unified various tribal associations and fragmented states. The Three kingdom period (57 BC – 668 AD) lasted for about 300 years until they were replaced by Unified Silla in the South and Balhae in the North. The coexistence of the Unified Silla and Balhae is referred to the period of the North and South (669-918 AD). Unified Silla came to an end, as it was replaced by the Goryeo dynasty (918-1392 AD) in the early 10th century. The Goryeo kingdom was later succeeded by the Joseon dynasty that came to rule the Korean peninsula until the turn of 20th century.

This chapter provides a brief overview of ancient kingdoms on the Korean peninsula from Gojoseon (2333 BC-108 BC) to Unified Silla (668-935 AD), followed by a summary of some selected K-dramas relevant to the historical period.

Two surviving historical documents provide valuable insights into Korea's ancient kingdoms. They are Samguk-sagi (History of the Three Kingdoms) and Samguk-yusa (Memorabilia of the Three Kingdoms). The first record was written in 1145 by Kim Pu-sik, a high court official of the Goryeo dynasty. The second historical account was written in 1279 by the Korean Buddhist monk, Iryon. From the 13th century onward, the court of the Joseon kingdom kept detailed recordings of the reign of each monarch. The multi-volume records (known as the Veritable Records of the Joseon dynasty) contain diaries of daily activities, written by the Office of Royal Decrees (Sungjongwon), a state organ in charge of all state documents (Seth 2006).

Gojoseon (2333BC-108BC)

According to Samguk-yusa, Gojoseon was recorded as the earliest Korean kingdom that was established on October 3rd in 2333 BC. Every year, Koreans celebrate their almost 5000-year-old history on October 3, as "gaecheonjeol" (the National Foundation Day 개천절).

K-drama on the Pre-Gojoseon Era		
The TV series drama, Arthdal Chronicles (아스달 연대기) is a fictional prehistoric drama. It depicts ancient tribes tracing back to the era of hunting and gathering societies.		
	Title	Arthdal Chronicles (아스달 연대기)
	Production	Released in 2019
	Cast	Song Joong-gi, Jang Dong-gun
	Synopsis	The drama tells a story about the life of various ancient tribes in a fictional land called Arth. Eunsome, a half-human and a half Neanderthal, tries to save the Wahan tribe of hunters and gatherers that raised him, against other powerful tribes of agricultural settlers armed with weapons. (poster © TvN/ Netflix).

Koreans trace their ancestry to Tangun, the founder of Gojoseon. All Korean children learn the founding mythology of Gojoseon and the Korean nation at school. Samguk-yusa describes the creation mythology of Gojoseon as follows:

Hwanin's son, Hwanung, wished to descend from Heaven and live in the world of human beings. Knowing his son's desire, Hwanin surveyed the three highest mountains and found Mount Taebaek the most suitable place for his son to settle and help human beings. Therefore, he gave Hwanung three heavenly seals and dispatched him to rule over the people. Hwanung descended with three thousand followers to a spot under a tree by the Holy Altar stop Mount Taebaek, and he called this place the City of God. He was the Heavenly King of Hwanung. Leading the Earl of Wind, the Master of Rain, and the Master of Clouds, he took charge of some three hundred and sixty areas of responsibility, including agriculture, allotted life spans, illness, punishment, and good and evil, and brought culture to his people. At that time a bear and a tiger living in the same cave prayed to Holy Hwanung to transform them into human beings. He gave them a bundle of sacred mugworts and twenty cloves of garlic and said, "If you eat these and shun the sunlight for one hundred days, you will assume human form." Both animals ate the species and avoided the sun. After twenty-one days the bear became a woman but the tiger, unable to observe the taboo, remained a tiger. Unable to find a husband, the bear-woman prayed under the altar tree for a child. Hwanung metamorphosed himself, lay with her, and begot a son called Tangun Wanggom. (cited in Seth 2006: 24)

According to Samguk-yusa, Tangun Wanggom was the son of Hwanung and a bear-woman. The demi-god, Tangun, then founded the kingdom of Gojoseon and chose Asadal (somewhere in present-day Manchuria and North Korea) as the capital city of his kingdom.

Gojoseon began as a tribal federation and developed into a powerful kingdom. While diverse ethnic groups lived in Gojoseon, the ruling house of Gojoseon was mostly dominated by ethnic Koreans. For many centuries,

Gojoseon occupied a vast territory, covering todays' North Korea and Manchuria.

Map 1.1 Gojoseon

Between 109-108 BC, the Han Empire in the northern territory (present-day China) launched military campaigns against Gojoseon (Seth 2006:18). During the same time period, the ruling house of Gojoseon changed to non-Korean ethnic groups. As the ruling house of Gojoseon lost its control over Gojoseon's constituent tribes, the kingdom fragmented into numerous smaller states (Puyo, Okcho, Umno, Ye, Nakrang-guk, Dongye, Guda-guk, Galsa-guk, Gaema-guk, Goguryo and Hangin-guk) (KOCIS 2019). The northwestern part of Gojoseon was incorporated into the Chinese Han empire, as it came under the direct control of administrative units called commanderies. Meanwhile, other post-Gojoseon states existed as tributary states of China's Han Empire. The post-Gojoseon period was marked by a century-long existence of numerous mini-states or tribal federations warring against each other within the framework of the hegemonic rule of the Han Empire.

The Han Empire of China exerted great influence all over Asia. It kept many tributary states including Vietnam and Korea within the China-centered imperial system (Seth 2006: 18). In return for their loyalty and cooperation, the tributary states received prestigious cultural goods from the Han royal court and permission to trade with China (Seth 2006: 19). The Han Empire spread Chinese scripts as the means of written communications among its tributary states. With its rule over Asia for about 400 years, the Han Empire also disseminated Buddhism and Confucianism all over Asia. As the Han Empire developed the system of governance based on Confucian political philosophy, all tributary kingdoms followed China by adopting the Confucian model of political system[1].

In many ways, the Han Empire (206 BC-220 AD) is comparable to the Roman Empire (27 BC -476 AD) in Europe. The Roman Emperor ruled over various kings of its tributary kingdoms in Europe and Asia Minor. Similar to the Han Empire in China, the Roman Empire spread Christianity as its state religion and the use of Latin language as the main language of written communication among its constituent kingdoms.

K-drama on the post-Gojoseon kingdoms

Due to the scarcity of historical records on Gojoseon, the dramatization of the Gojoseon era is extremely difficult. A few K-dramas, however, shed light on historical events relating to the demise of Gojoseon and the post-Gojoseon period of warring states, leading up to the emergence of the three kingdoms (Goguryeo, Baekje, and Silla) on the Korean peninsula. Two TV series, "Jumong" and "Princess Jamyeong-go", depict inter-state rivalry among many fragmented states during the post-Gojoseon period.

---

[1] Confucianism refers to ideas of Confucius (551-479 AD) in China. Confucianism remained the principal basis for moral, social, and political philosophy in Korea until the end of the 19th century.

	Title	Jumong (주몽)
	Production	Released in 2006 (82 episodes)
		Song Il-gook, Han Hye-jin
	Synopsis	"Jumong" deals with power struggle in the royal court of Puyo, one of many warring-states after the collapse of Gojoseon. It portrays the political processes whereby the founder of Goguryeo, Jumong, brought many states under the control of his kingdom (poster © MBC).

"Princess Jamyeong-go" is a historical fusion drama, drawing on the legendary story of a mystical drum in Nakrang-guk, a small kingdom during the post-Gojoseon period. According to the story recorded in Samguk-yusa, the drum (called "Jamyeongo") had the power to make alert sounds whenever the country's border is breached by foreign invaders. As the story goes, a princess of Nakrang fell in love with a prince of Goguryeo. Upon her lover's request, the princess destroyed the legendary drum and Goguryeo came to conquer Nakrang-guk. Inspired by the legendary story of the drum, the TV series, "Princess Jamyeong-go", tells a fictional story of love triangle involving two princesses of Nakrang-guk and the prince of Goguryeo.

	Title	Princess Jameyong-go
	Production	2009 (39 episodes)
	Cast	Park Min-young, Jung Ryeo-won, Jung Kyung-ho
	Synopsis	Two sisters, both princesses of Nakrang-guk, love the same person, a prince of Goguryeo, the archenemy of Nakrang-guk. They must choose between love and loyalty. (poster © SBS).

The Three Kingdom Period (57 BC - 668 AD)

While the northern part of the Korean peninsula was dominated by Gojoseon and later post-Gojoseon kingdoms, the southern area was ruled by confederations of tribes including Mahan, Jinhan, and Byeonhan, collectively known as the tree Han tribal states. The confederacy of Kaya, which was established in the area of former Byeonhan, existed for many centuries until it was incorporated into more powerful neighboring states such as Silla and Baekje. Meantime, the former Mahan area was incorporated into the Baekje kingdom, while the former Jinhan territory came under the rule of the Silla kingdom. Further to the southern Korean peninsula was the Tamna kingdom located on the present-day Jeju island.

In the 1st century BC, the fragmented states on the Korean peninsula came under the rule of three powerful kingdoms, called Goguryeo, Baekje and Silla. According to Samguk-sagi, the oldest written document on Korean history, Silla was founded in 57 BC, Goguryeo in 37 BC, and Baekje in 18 BC (Seth 2006: 27). While the period between 1st century BC and 7th century AD is known as the "Three Kingdom period", this characterization overlooks the existence of two smaller kingdoms such as Kaya and Tamna.

Cultural and economic exchanges across borders greatly facilitated the spread of Buddhism and Confucianism on the Korean peninsula. Buddhist monks and Confucian scholars from all three kingdoms frequently travelled to China and brought various cultural and religious artifacts with them. The Chinese writing system was adopted as the means of written communication among the ruling elites in all three kingdoms (Seth 2006).

After the powerful Han Empire of China went into decline by 220 AD, China once more fragmented into many warring states that lasted more than three centuries (Seth 2006). With the demise of the Han Empire in the 3rd century AD, the three kingdoms on the Korean peninsula enjoyed greater autonomy from China and expanded their territories.

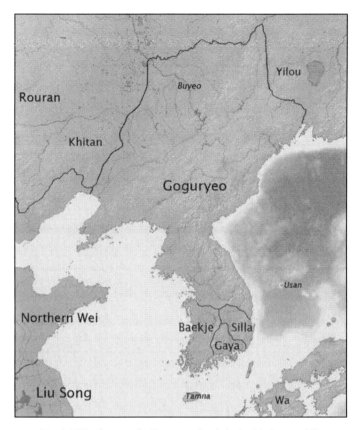

Map 1.2 Kingdoms on the Korean peninsula in the 5th Century AD

Goguryeo (37 BC – 668)

Jumong founded the Kingdom of Goguryeo in 37 B.C. and expanded its territory by absorbing neighboring states including Buyeo (or Puyo), Jolbon, and Nakrang-guk. For many centuries, Goguryeo remained as a formidable military power. In the early 5th century, King Gwanggaeto (r. 391-413 AD) further expanded Goguryeo's territory and exerted control over the northern part of the Korean Peninsula including Manchuria and parts of Inner Mongolia (KOCIS 2019).

K-dramas and Movies on Goguryeo

Several K-dramas depict historical events and legendary figures relating to the Goguryeo kingdom. They include: Jumong (주몽), The Kingdom of the Wind (바람의 나라), Jamyeong-go (자명고), The Legend (태왕사신기), King Gwanggaeto the Great (광개토태왕), The Great Hero (Yeon Gaesomun 연개소문), Sword and Flower (칼과꽃) and Dae Jo-young (대조영).

The Kingdom of the Wind (바람의 나라) focuses on historical events during the reign of the 2nd and 3rd king of Goguryeo. It centres around the life of Daewang-mushin (대왕무신), the third king of Goguryeo.

	Title	The Kingdom of the Wind
	Production	Aired in 2008 (36 episodes)
	Cast	Song Il-guk, Choi Jung-won
	Synopsis	A prince was born with a prophecy that he would become a person who would endanger the Goguryeo kingdom. Although his life was spared, he grew up outside the royal court without knowing his true identity. The drama tells a fictional story about how he becomes the third king of Goguryeo (poster © KBS).

Two TV series dramas, "The Legend" (태왕사신기) and "King Gwanggaeto the Great", both deal with the life of the 19th King of Goguryeo, King Gwanggaeto the Great.

	Title	King Gwanggaeto the Great
	Production	Aired in 2011 (92episodes)
	Cast	Lee Tae-gon, In Hye-lee
	Synopsis	It is a historical action drama, based on the life of the 19th King of Goguryeo, Gwanggaeto the Great (poster © KBS).

The TV series, "Yeongae Somun", depicts Goguryeo's military prowess, focusing on one of Goguryeo's powerful military generals. Another TV series, The Great Hero, also depicts the life of Yeon Gaesomun.

Title	Yeongae Somun
Production	Aired in 2006-2007 (100 episodes)
Cast	Yoo Dong-geun, Na Han-il, Hwang In-yong
Synopsis	While loosely based on some real historical events, the drama contains many fictional stories about the child and youthhood of Yeongae Somun, especially regarding his relationship with Silla's general, Kim Yushin. (poster © sbs)

In 589 AD, China was reunified under the powerful Sui dynasty that began military campaigns against Goguryeo. In 612 AD, the Sui Dynasty mobilized more than a million troops to attack Goguryeo. Under the leadership of General Eulji Mundeok, Goguryeo defeated the Chinese forces in the famous battle of Salsu (살수대첩) where only 2,700 Chinese soldiers out of one million troops were reportedly to have survived. Greatly weakened by its military setbacks, the Sui Dynasty was replaced by a new empire, called the Tang dynasty in 618 AD (Seth 2006).

Goguryeo played a pivotal role in spreading Buddhism and Chinese classics to other kingdoms in Korea. In 372 AD, Goguryeo adopted Buddhism as the state religion. In the same year, Goguryeo established Taehak, a state-sponsored educational institute, to promote higher learning (Seth 2006:35). Taehak is the predecessor to Sungkyungwan, the highest learning institution of the Joseon kingdom.

Baekje (18 BC -660 AD)

According to Samguk-sagi, the two stepsons of Jumong established the kingdom of Baekje (or Paekje). Although Jumong's second wife, the leader of a small tribal state Jolbon, played a crucial role in founding the Goguryeo kingdom, Jumong passed the throne to Yuri, his own son from his first marriage. Seeking to build their own kingdom, Jumong's second wife and her two sons moved to the south-western part of the Korean peninsula and established the Kingdom of Baekje in 18 BC.

During the reign of Geunchogo (r. 346-375 AD), Baekje saw its heydays. Carrying out a territorial expansion policy, King Geunchogo conquered the Mahan federation that existed in the southern coastal area. Baekje launched a military campaign against Goguryeo in 371 AD and conquered some parts of Goguryeo's territory.

K-dramas and movies on Baekje

Several dramas depict historical events concerning the Baekje kingdom. They include: King Geunchogo, The King's Daughter, Soo Baek-hyang, Ballade of Seo Dong, and Gyebaek: The Great King's Dream. The TV series drama, "King Geunchogo", is about the life of the 13th king of Baekje, Geunchogo. Under his reign, the Baekje kingdom saw its heydays, as it ruled the vast area of the Korean peninsula and beyond, including some territories of former Goguryeo and present-day China.

Title	King Geunchogo
Production	Aired in 2010-2011 (60 episodes)
Cast	Kam Woo-sung, Kim Ji-soo, Lee Jong-won
Synopsis	The drama depicts the life of the warrior king, Geun Chogo, who expanded Baekje's territory by conquering Mahan and part of Kaya and Goguryeo. (poster © KBS)

The TV series, Ballade of Seodong, is about King Mu, the 30th King of Baekje (r. 600-641).

	Title	Ballade of Seo Dong
	Aired	2005-2006 (55 episodes)
	Cast	Jo Hyeon-jae, Lee Bo-yeong
	Synopsis	The drama tells a story based on the folksong recorded in Samguk-yusa. According to the historical document, Seodong, a commoner, succeeded in marrying Princess Seonhwa, the daughter of King Jinpyeong (r. 579-632) by spreading a folksong containing rumours about the princess. The couple then moved to Baekje where they rose to the royal ruler of the kingdom. (poster © SBS)

Thanks to its fertile agricultural lands, the new kingdom, Baekje, became an economically and culturally prosperous society. Baekje's pottery and ceramics were considered one of the finest during the Three Kingdom period and Baekje had a rich stock of highly developed arts and architecture. Like Goguryeo, Baekje adopted Buddhism as its state religion in 384 AD. King Mu (r. 600-641 AD) built Miruk temple, the largest Buddhist temple in East Asia. Baekje forged close diplomatic and cultural ties with the Wa (Wae) in Japan. Baekje disseminated its cultural traditions, including architecture and pottery techniques, to Japan that had a friendly diplomatic relationship with Baekje.

Silla (57 BC – 668 AD)

The kingdom of Silla was established in 57 BC in the south-eastern part of the Korean peninsula. Unlike other Korean kingdoms, Silla had experienced the reign of three female monarchs[2]. With no other Korean kingdoms governed by female sovereigns, the rule of female monarchs underscores the importance of Silla's strict caste system of blood lineage. Silla's political system was marked by a strict caste system, known as the "bone-rank" system (골품제도).

Table 1. 1 The "bone-rank" system

| seongol (성골 sacred bone) |
| jingol (진골 true bone) |
| Doopoom (두품 Head Ranks) |

The bone-rank system categorized people according to their bloodlines. The hereditary "bone rank" system limited people's access to special privileges such as qualification for office. The top bone-rank was the seongol (성골 sacred bone) that consisted of only the members of the royal Kim clan. Silla limited the succession to the throne to only the members of the "sacred bone" rank. The next highest rank was the jingol (진골 true bone) that included the members of powerful aristocratic families such as the Park and Sok royal consort families, and the royal house of Pon Kaya.

When King Chinyong died in 632 AD, leaving no male heir, his eldest daughter (later Seondeok) was chosen to succeed him. Female members of the sacred bone were allowed to govern, only when no males of the sacred bone rank could assume the throne. The reign of Queen Seondeok (r. 632-647) was followed by the reign of another female monarch. Since Queen Seondeok had no child of her own, she chose her cousin, Jindeok, to assume the throne. When Queen Jindeok (r. 647-654 AD) died in 654 AD, without leaving any male heir, the sacred-bone rank became almost extinct. Consequently, monarchs were drawn from the second highest rank, Jingol.

The jingol class had access to the highest offices in the government and could serve on the Council of Notables (화백 Hwabaek), the highest political decision-making body after the monarch. The Hwabaek council deliberated on the most important matters of state, such as succession to the throne and the declaration of war. Only the powerful aristocrats with jingol lineage

---

[2] The last female ruler of Silla was Queen Jinsong (r. 887-898) who briefly governed Unified Silla in the end of 9th century.

could sit on the council (Seth 2006). In addition, only members of Jingol could take part in the Hwarang (화랑), the royal elite guard made of sons from aristocratic families. The Hwarang had its own military academy that trained aristocratic youth in martial arts and Confucian classics. Most of the prominent military and political figures of Silla, such as General Kim Yu-shin, served in their youth as Hwarang members (Han 1995; Seth 2006).

K-dramas and films on Silla

Several K-dramas depict court intrigues over the accession to the throne in Silla. For instance, they include "Queen Seondeok" and "Hwarang: the beginning".

	Title	Queen Seondeok
	Production	Aired in 2009 (62 episodes)
	Synopsis	The TV drama, Queen Seondeok, is about the early history of Silla with a focus on the power struggle between Lady Mishil and Princess Deok Man (later Queen Seon Deok, the first female monarch of Silla). (poster © mbc)
	Cast	Lee Yo Won, Go Hyun-jung, Uhm Tae-woong

Albeit largely based on a fictional story about the Silla's game of the throne, the drama does make references to real historical events involving Lady Mishil, Queen Seondeok (r. 632-647 AD), , and General Kim Yu-shin (595-673). Lady Mishil, a member of the True Bone caste, was the consort of King Jinheung. General Kim Yu-shin, one of Silla's most powerful military generals, later succeeded to the throne.

The third highest rank was "yukdoopoom (head-rank-six)", consisted of members of other aristocratic families, whose members could hold the middle-level offices (Seth 2006: 39-40).

> **Hwarang**
>
> The TV series drama depicting the life of the ruling class of the Silla kingdom is "Hwarang: The Beginning".
>
> | | | |
> |---|---|---|
> | | Title | Hwarang 2017 |
> | | Production | Aired in 2017 (20 episodes) |
> | | Cast | Park Seo-joon, Go Ah-ra, Park Hyeong-sik, Min ho. |
> | | Synopsis | The drama tells a fictional love story among members of Hwarang, the elite guard of aristocratic youth in the Silla kingdom. (poster © KBS) |
>
> Mostly fictional love stories involving the crown prince and some prominent youths from powerful aristocratic families, the drama depicts the origin of Hwarang, the powerful military organization of aristocratic youths.

Kaya (42 – 532 AD)

The kingdom of Kaya (or Gaya) existed in the form of a confederacy of tribal states. The Kaya confederacy (also known as Gaya or Karak) consisted of six polities including Pon Kaya (original Kaya) and Dae-Kaya (greater Kaya). Kaya's creation mythology was recorded in the 11th century historical work, Garak Gookgi. According to Garak Gookgi, the kings of the Kaya confederacy emerged from golden eggs that descended from heaven (Seth 2006).

Kaya had rich iron deposits and fertile agricultural land, in addition to its optimal maritime location. The iron production made Kaya an important hub of commerce and industry in East Asia, linking China, Japan, and India (Seth 2006). Despite its prosperity and commercial success, the Kaya confederacy fell victim to the military ambition of its neighboring kingdoms (Baekje and Silla). The Kaya confederacy fell apart as its constituent units were gradually annexed by its powerful neighbor Silla. Conquering Pon Kaya in 532 and Tae Kaya in 562, Silla completely annexed Kaya by the mid- 6th century (Seth 2006; Pratt and Rutt 1999; KOCIS 2019).

K-Drama on Kaya

The only TV drama series that depicts the Kaya federation is "Kim Soo-ro" which was aired in 2010. The drama portrays the political processes leading to the emergence of Geumgwan Kaya, the most powerful state of the Kaya confederacy, that dominated sea trade and iron working. The TV series sheds light on the importance of iron-making and international trade in the Kaya confederacy.

	Title	Kim Soo-ro, the Iron King
	Production	Aired in 2010 (32 episodes)
	Cast	Ji Sung as Kim Soo-ro
	Synopsis	The drama tells a fictional story about the life of Kim Soo-ro, the leader of Pon Kaya. It depicts power struggle between Kim Soo-ro and his opponents including his half-brother and leaders of rival tribes. (poster © mbc)

The End of the Three Kingdoms and the Emergence of the North-South Period (7th --10th Century)

The relationship between all three kingdoms (Goguryeo, Silla and Baekje) was based on intense competition and rivalry, as they were often at war with each other over territorial disputes. Baekje attacked Goguryeo and expanded its territory further to the north. In retaliation, Goguryeo helped Silla to conquer a portion of Baekje's territory, by the end of the 4th century. In return, Baekje mounted military assaults on Silla, ironically with the help of its former enemy, Goguryeo. Between 433 AD and 553 AD, Baekje formed an alliance with Silla against Goguryeo. The alliance ended after Silla occupied parts of Baekje territory. Fighting against Silla, Baekje turned to Goguryeo for help. In retaliation, Silla then made an alliance with China's Tang dynasty to counter Baekje and Goguryeo.

Goguryeo versus Tang

The film, "The Great Battle" (Ansi Fortress 안시성), depicts the epic battle of the inhabitants of Goguryeo's Ansi Fortress against the 200,000 invading troops led by China's Tang Dynasty. It is famous for its excellent cinematographic portrayal of battle scenes.

	Title	The Great Battle
	Production	2018 (Director: Kim Gwang-sik)
	Cast	Jo In-sung and Nam Ju-hyuk
	Synopsis	In 645AD, the Tang Dynasty invaded Goguryeo. This drama focuses on the famous battle at the Ansi Fortress in Goguryeo. Although the Tang forces outnumbered the Goguryeo army, the movie depicts how the people in the Ansi fortress overcame their numeric disadvantage with ingenious military tactics. (poster © next entertainment world)

During the reign of Uija (r. 641-660 AD), Baekje fell to the joint attacks from the Tang-Silla forces. The Baekje king was taken to China together with hundreds and thousands of prisoners of war. The joint military aggression by

Tang and Silla ended with the defeat of Goguryeo in 668 AD. King Pojang of Goguryeo was also taken hostage to China (Pratt and Rutt 1999).

With the two rival kingdoms defeated, the Tang dynasty in China took over Goguryeo and Baekje, and tried to control even Silla, its former ally. In response, Silla fought against the Tang and succeeded in keeping the former Baekje territory under Silla's control. Significant portions of the former Goguryeo territory were, however, lost to Tang, until a new Korean kingdom, called Balhae, emerged from the land that previously belonged to Goguryeo.

The Demise of Baekje

The TV series drama, "Gyebaek", tells the story about general Gyebaek and the political processes leading to the fall of Baekje kingdom.

	Title	Gyebaek (or Kyebaek)
	Production	Aired in 2011 (36 episodes)
	Cast	Lee Seo-jin
	Synopsis	The drama portrays the life of General Gyebaek who led the famous battle of Hawangsanbeol against the Tang-Silla invaders. In 660 AD, Silla's General Kim Yu-sin defeated Baekje troops led by General Gyebaek in the battle. (poster © mbc)

In addition, some films shed light on the political situation at the end of the Three Kingdom period. For instance, the films, "Hwangsanbeol (황산벌)" and "Pyongyangsung (평양성)" deal with Silla's military campaigns against Baekje and Goguryeo

---

Table 1.2 Changing Military Alliances and Major Political Events between

Year (AD)	Military Alliance & Conflicts and other Political Events
220	The Han Empire broke up into smaller warring states.
589	The Sui dynasty was established in China.
612	The Sui dynasty attacked Goguryeo with one million troops, but its military campaign failed.
618	The Sui dynasty was replaced by the Tang dynasty in China.
645	The Tang invaded Goguryeo but failed to conquer it.
660	The Tang-Silla allied forces defeated Baekje.
668	The Tang-Silla joint forces defeated Goguryeo.

With the help of Tang China, Silla defeated both Baekje and Goguryeo in the late 7th century. Now that their common rivals were gone, the Tang wanted to control the entire Korean peninsula in the form of old-style commanderies. The Chinese emperor demanded that the Silla king would take a subordinate position, as the head of a Chinese commandery, rather than staying as a sovereign monarch. Rejecting Tang's demand, Silla instead waged a war against Tang. Shilla drove out the Tang forces from the former Baekje territory by 671 AD and gained control of some parts of the former Goguryeo territory by 676 AD.

While Silla occupied most of the southern part of the Korean peninsula, the people under Tang-controlled former Goguryeo eventually rebelled against the Tang dynasty. In 698 AD, the rebels founded the kingdom of Balhae (or Parhae) and exerted control over the former Goguryeo territory including the north-east coastal region.

Between the late 7th century and the early 10th century, the two kingdoms, Balhae in the north and Unified Silla in the south, coexisted on the Korean peninsula (Pratt, and Rutt, 1999). The North-South states period (Nambook Sidae 남북시대), during which Korea was divided into two kingdoms (Unified Silla and Balhae), lasted for more than 200 years.

Table 1.1 K-dramas and films on the Three Kingdoms and Kaya

Time	K-dramas and Films
Post-Gojoseon	Jumong, Jamyeong-go
Silla (57 BC-668AD)	Hwarang (화랑), Queen Seondeok (선덕여왕), Hwangsanbeol (황산벌), Pyeongyangsung (평양성)
Goguryeo (37 BC-668 AD)	Jumong (주몽), The Kingdom of the Wind (바람의 나라), Jamyeong-go (자명고), The Legend (태왕사신기), King Gwanggaeto the Great (광개토태왕), The Great Hero (Yeon Gaesomun 연개소문), Sword and Flower (칼과꽃). Dae Jo-young (대조영).
Baekje (18 BC -660 AD)	King Geun Chogo (근초고왕), The King's Daughter, Soo Baek-hyang (왕의딸 백수향), Ballade of Seo Dong (서동요), Gyebaek: The Great King's Dream (계백), Thousand Years of Love (천년지애)
Kaya (42-532 AD)	Kim Soo-ro (김수로)

Unified Silla (668-935 AD)

Unified Shilla eventually restored bilateral economic and cultural relations with the Tang dynasty. The rewarming of the bilateral relationship was necessitated by the rise of Balhae, the successor state of the former Goguryeo kingdom. As Silla and Tang were both threatened by Balhae, they normalized their diplomatic relations in 733 AD. Between the 8th and 9th century, the amicable relationship between Unified Silla and Tang enabled frequent bilateral, commercial and cultural exchanges (Seth 2006: 63). While traders, monks, and scholars from Silla frequently traveled to Tang, many Koreans studied in the Imperial Academy of Tang or in Buddhist monasteries, and some Koreans even served in the Chinese government and its army (Pratt, and Rutt, 1999: 460). Unified Silla adopted Confucianism, a political philosophy imported from China. Since Confucianism emphasizes filial piety, loyalty to the ruler, and respect for authority, among other ethical values, it served as a useful ideological tool to instil the loyalty of its subjects to the monarch. During this period, Unified Silla enjoyed the greatest maritime activity in Korea's history, as Korean merchants dominated seaborne trade in north-east Asia (Seth 2006).

By the late 9th century, however, Silla went into political decline, as it was embroiled in political violence resulting from the corruption in the government and the emergence of powerful local warlords (Pratt and Rutt 1999). As the central government became weaker and weaker, the countryside was plagued by banditry and the rebellions of the suffering peasants. In 889 AD, a peasant rebellion broke out due to the excessive dual burden of taxation and corvée (mandatory unpaid labor for the state). As the rebellion spread across the country, the power struggle in the royal court, fueled by rivalry among aristocratic families, intensified and eventually resulted in the break-up of Unified Silla (Pratt and Rutt 1999).

K-dramas and Movies on Unified Silla

The TV series, "Emperor of the Sea (해신)", sheds light on Unified Silla's dominance in maritime commerce in the 9th century. The drama is based on the real historical figure, General Jang Bo-go who established a forward operating base (a military garrison) in Cheonghaejin (present-day Wando in South Korea). General Jang protected international maritime commerce with Asian countries by repelling pirates from his maritime garrison. (KOCIS 2019; Seth 2006)

Title	The Emperor of the Sea (해신)
Production	Aired in 2005 (51 episodes)
Cast	Choi Soo-jong, Chae Si-ra, Song Il-gook
Synopsis	The drama tells the story of General Jang Bo-go who was born as a slave in Unified Silla. He emigrated to China's Tang where he became a military officer. After returning to Unified Silla, he rose to the position of a powerful maritime lord with the possession of his own private navy. (poster © kbs)

The movie, "The Legend of Evil Lake," is a fantasy, horror film with the 9th century Unified Silla as its historical backdrop.

	Title	The Legend of Evil Lake
	Production	Released in 2003 (Directed by Lee Gwang-hoon)
	Cast	Jung Joon-ho
	Synopsis	Set in the time period of Queen Jingseong' reign in Unified Silla, the film tells a fictional fantasy story about a mysterious sword that would unleash vengeful spirits of a tribe that was massacred by the founder of the Silla kingdom. (poster © 2003 cinema service)

Between 901 and 936, Unified Silla fragmented into three competing kingdoms (Silla, Later Baekje, and Later Goguryeo). In 892, Gyeon-hwon (a peasant leader) established Later Baekje (후백제), while Gungye (a monk) founded Later Goguryeo (후고구려) in 901. In 934 AD, the last king of Silla abdicated and recognized Wang Gun as his successor (Seth 2006:71).

The Demise of Unified Silla		
The TV series, "Emperor Wang Gun", depicts power struggle among break-away states at the end of the Unified Silla period.		
	Title	Emperor Wang Gun
	Production	2000-2002 (200 episodes)
	Cast	Choi Soo-jong, Kim Yong-chul
	Synopsis	Gungye established "Later Goguryeo", a break-away kingdom from Unified Silla. Wang Gun initially helped Gungye but established a new kingdom, called Goryeo by taking over "Later Baekje" and the rest of Unified Silla. (poster © kbs)

In 935, Later Baekje succumbed to the powerful Goryeo kingdom. The precarious period of political instability, referred to the Later Three Kingdoms (후삼국시대) era, lasted until Wang Gun brought the three kingdoms under control of the new kingdom of Goryeo (or Koryo) in 936 AD. The name of Goryeo signifies that Goryeo is the successor state of the former Goguryeo (or Koguryeo).

Balhae (698-926 AD)

The kingdom of Balhae (or Parhae) was established by Dae Jo-young in 698 AD. As in the case with Gojoseon and other ancient Korean kingdoms, Balhae consisted of diverse non-Korean ethnic groups including various tribes in Manchuria (Seth 2006). Balhae's ruling house was, however, dominated by ethnic Koreans who emphasized their claim to Goguryeo's heritage (Pratt, and Rutt 1999).

K-dramas and Movies on Balhae

The TV series, Dae Jo-young(대조영), depicts the fall of Goguryeo and the rise of Balhae. Set at the time period between the mid 7th and early 8th century, the drama is based on the life story of Dae Jo-young, the founder of the Balhae Kingdom.

	Title	Dae Jo-young
	Production	Aired in 2007 (108 episodes)
	Cast	Choi Soo-jong, Park Ye-jin
	Synopsis	This TV series drama is about Dae Jo-yeong, the founder of Balhae kingdom. It depicts the early history of Balhae's creation (poster © KBS).

Balhae ruled the northern part of the Korean peninsular and beyond for more than two centuries. Balhae regained control over most of Goguryeo's former territory and defended it against Tang, as in the case with Balhae's naval attack on Tang in 732 AD. China's Tang dynasty tried to contain Balhae's rise in 733 by allying with Silla but their military mission was largely unsuccessful (Seth 2006: 67).

Balhae reached the height of its power in the 9th century under the reign of King Tae-Insu. As Balhae became a formidable power, the people of Tang China called Balhae "Haedong seongguk" (prosperous country in the east) (Pratt, and Rutt 1999: 340). Balhae established a bilateral relationship with the Tang dynasty for trade and cultural exchanges. At the same time, Balhae sought to maintain its independence by actively engaging with other countries including Japan. Therefore, Balhae maintained close economic and military ties with the Yamato government in Japan.

The Fall of Balhae		
A cinematographic film, "Shadowless sword", tells a story about the last prince of the Balhae Kingdom and his battle against the Khitan that eventually destroyed Balhae.		
	Title	Shadowless Sword
	Production	Released in 2005 (Directed by Kim Young-jun / Written by Kim Tae-kwan and Shin Joon-hee)
	Cast	Lee Soe-jin, Yoon So-yi
	Synopsis	The film is based on a fictional story about a swordswoman who tried to protect the last member of Balhae's royal family from the invading Khitans. (poster © taewon entertainment)

In the early 10th century, Balhae collapsed due to persistent invasions led by northern tribes in Manchuria. In 926 AD, the Khitan, a seminomadic tribe in Manchuria, invaded Balhae (KOCIS 2019). Overthrowing Balhae, the Khitan established the Liao dynasty and continued its military campaigns by also attacking Tang China (Pratt and Rutt 1999). Eventually, the weakened Tang Empire broke up into smaller warring states (Seth 2006: 68).

Table 1.3 Military Alliance & Conflicts between 7th and 10th century

Year AD	Military Alliance & Conflicts
732	Balhae attacked the Tang dynasty.
733	Tang-Unified Silla attacked Balhae
892	Unified Silla disintegrated into warring-sates. Gyeon Hwon established "Later Baekje" (a splinter state of Unified Silla).
901	Goongye established "Later Goguryeo" (another splinter state of Unified Silla).
926	The Khitan defeated Balhae and established the Liao dynasty. The Khitan attacked the Tang dynasty.
934	Unified Silla was defeated by Later Goguryeo.
936	The kingdom of Goryeo was established.

Chapter 2

Goryeo Kingdom (918-1392)

In 918 AD, Wang Gun (later King Taejo) founded the Goryeo dynasty and expanded the frontier of Goryeo further to the north (to the Chongchon river). To the south, he incorporated the island of Tamna (present-day Jeju island of South Korea) into the Goryeo kingdom in 938 AD (Pratt and Rutt, 1999).

The early Goryeo kingdom was based on an alliance of warlords and powerful families of the previous Silla aristocracy, as Wang Gun tried to secure his position by forging a marriage alliance. Thus, he came to have 29 wives, including one from the Silla's royal clan and 23 from powerful aristocratic families (Pratt, and Rutt, 1999:504). Ironically, the marriage alliance came to undermine the power of the monarch as it resulted in power rivalry among numerous princes and their maternal families over the succession to the throne. When Wang Gun died in 943 AD, the royal court was divided by factional fights over the succession to the throne (Seth 2006:77). The state of political instability, resulting from the weak monarch and the powerful aristocracy, continued until the end of the 10th century. The situation, however, drastically changed under the reign of the fourth king of Goryeo, King Gwangjong (r. 949-975), who took various measures to strengthen the monarchical power.

First, he reduced the power of the aristocratic families by limiting the number of slaves that they owned. In addition, he issued a Slave Investigation Act in 956 AD that emancipated those who had been unfairly enslaved during the chaotic war period of the Later Three Kingdoms. The measure also benefited the state, as it turned the freed slaves into tax paying peasants (Seth 2006).

To consolidate monarchical control over the state, King Gwangjong established the state examination system in 958 AD[3]. Through the "gwageo" or the civil service examination, the state selected only the educated scholars or technicians with expert knowledge and appointed them to various posts in the government. Although the previous Silla kingdom experimented with the civil service exam, it was only by the 10th century that the examination developed into a significant selection tool to allocate members of the aristocratic elite to government offices (Seth 2006: 80).

Despite his progressive policies, his reign was marked with many bloody purges against his rivals in the court as well as his own family members and relatives. While carrying out bloody purges against his opponents and rivals, he created a large military force loyal to him. Due to the violent purges during his reign, King Gwang-jong earned the reputation for being a "violent and cruel king".

K-dramas on King Gwangjong		
The early period of Goryeo is depicted in several K-dramas. Among them, two dramas stand out for their different take on the King Gwang-jong. The TV series, "Shine or Go Crazy" and "Moon lovers: Scarlet Heart Ryeo" depict the life of King Gwangjong with a different focus on Gwangjong's political legacy.		
	Title	Shine or Go Crazy (aka Shine or Be Mad)
	Production	Aired in 2015 (24 episodes)
	Cast	Jang Hyuk, Oh Yeon-seo
	Synopsis	This drama is a fictional love story between Wang So (King Gwangjong of Goryeo) and Shin Yool (an exiled princess of Balhae). Their love story is interwoven with real stories based on historical events and power rivalry in the royal court. (poster © mbc)

---

[3] The civil examination system was first developed in China in the 1st century AD (Seth 2006).

Many Koreans regarded him as a progressive king, while some portray him as a ruthless ruler. As explained in the overview, King Gwangjong introduced many reform measures that ultimately shaped the governance system of the early Goryeo kingdom. He enforced the meritocratic civil service exam and drastically reduced the number of slaves. Gwangjong carried out a land reform and distributed land to farmers.

A historical fantasy drama, "Moon Lovers", is very popular especially among K-pop (Korean pop music) fans. The drama's cast included some well-known K-pop artists such as IU and Baekhyun from EXO, a boyband. The drama's OSTs (original soundtrack) feature many K-pop hits.

	Title	Moon Lovers: Scarlet Heart Ryeo
	Production	Aired in 2016 (20 episodes)
	Synopsis	It is a fantasy fusion drama. A girl from contemporary South Korea is transported to Goryeo in 941 AD. She falls in love with one of the princes competing for the throne. As she gets entangled in power struggle among the competing princes including Wang So (later King Gwangjong), she witnesses a series of bloody purges and court intrigues. (poster © sbs)
	Cast	Lee Joon Gi and IU.

The fifth king, Kyeongong (975-981 AD), further undermined the power of the aristocracy by giving fixed incomes to the government officials according to rank. The sixth king introduced a national academy, Gukjagam, which changed its name to Sungkyungwan in 992. In addition, the Goryeo government expanded its educational system by founding numerous hyanggyo (provincial colleges). These measures contributed to the transformation of Goryeo from an aristocratic confederation into a centralized state, staffed by officials selected through the civil service examinations (KOCIS 2019; Seth 2006).

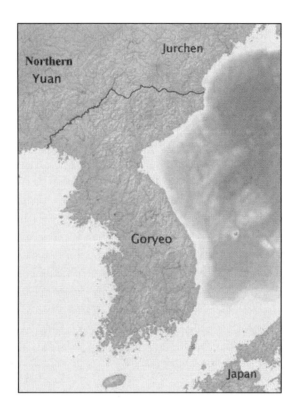

Map 2.1 Goryeo in 1374

Culture and Society

Goryeo's society was stratified into three social categories: yangban (aristocracy), pyeongmin (commoners), and cheonmin (the low-born). Yangban refers to mainly landowners and state bureaucrats that held positions in the government. Below yangban, there were pyeongmin (the commoners) that included farmers, merchants and skilled craftsmen. At the bottom of the social hierarchy existed cheonmin (the low-born) that included slaves and butchers. There were two types of slaves. Public slaves worked for government offices, schools and Buddhist temples, while private slaves belonged to yangban and some well-to-do pyeongmin. Most slaves were descendants of prisoners of wars or some heavily indebted commoners or in some cases, members of families who were involved in anti-government rebellions (Pratt, and Rutt 1999:429).

Women in Goryeo enjoyed a higher social status than their counterpart in the Joseon dynasty, the last kingdom of Korea. In Goryeo, women could inherit property from their parents as the inheritance was equally divided among siblings regardless of gender. Married women could keep their own property separate from their husbands' and could pass it on to their children. Thanks to women's property ownership, upper-class women enjoyed considerable power and independence. Reflecting the importance of women's wealth and power, matrilineal lineage was highly appreciated by the upper-class families. Goryeo had its unique marriage customs whereby the newly-wed men often resided in their wives' homes after marriage and demanded no bride wealth or dowry. Divorced or widowed women could remarry. Goryeo women could freely interact with men in public places. All these practices, unfortunately, came to an end in the neo-Confucian Joseon dynasty (Seth 2006: 92-93).

Buddhism exerted a great influence on Goryeo society. Wang Gun, the founder of the Goryeo dynasty, was a devoted Buddhist, and had ten temples built in Gaesong alone, the capital city of Goryeo (Pratt, and Rutt 1999:504). Thanks to Goryeo's excellent printing technology, the people of Goryeo produced the Tripitaka Koreana (a Korean collection of Buddhist scriptures) that was carved onto 81,258 wooden printing blocks. It should be noted that the people of Goryeo already invented metal printing types in 1377, more than 200 years before Johannes Gutenberg did in Europe. Unfortunately, during the long years of wars with the Khitans and the Mongols, many precious cultural heritages of Goryeo, including important historical documents and buildings such as the nine-tier pagoda at Hwangnyongsa Temple, were destroyed (KOCIS 2019).

Goryeo had an active trade relationship with its neighboring countries (the Song dynasty in China, various tribal states in Central Asia, and Japan) as well as with some countries in Southeast Asia and even Arabia (KOCIS 2019). Goryeo's active engagement in commercial and cultural exchanges with foreign countries made a significant contribution to the enrichment of Goryeo's culture.

Foreign Invasions

Between the 10th and the 12th century, multi-ethnic China saw the emergence of several competing dynasties including the Song, the Liao (the Khitan), and the Jin (the Jurchen). During the period of warring states in China, Goryeo and Balhae faced numerous invasions from the competing kingdoms in China. First, the Khitan, a semi-nomadic tribe in Manchuria, invaded and defeated Balhae in 926. The Liao dynasty (916-1125), established by the Khitan in Manchuria, launched military campaigns against the Song dynasty (960-1279) in China and its ally on the Korean peninsula, the Goryeo kingdom (Seth 2006). Goryeo eventually became a tributary state to the Liao dynasty and remained under the influence of the Liao dynasty until 1054.

In the early 12th century, the Jurchen, a tribe in Manchuria, began to challenge the Khitan. Allied with the Song dynasty, the Jurchen defeated the Khitan's Liao dynasty. Between 1103 and 1109, the Jurchen and Goryeo were engaged in military conflicts that ended with the Jurchen's partial victory. In 1115, the Jurchen established the state of Jin (1115-1234) and began attacking the weakened Song dynasty in China. By 1126, Goryeo was forced to enter into a tributary relationship with the Jurchen's Jin dynasty (Seth 2006). But Goryeo's relationship with the Jurchen did not last long as the Mongols emerged as the new ruler of China.

In the early 13th century, the Mongols conquered the Jin Dynasty (Jurchen) of China and established the Yuan dynasty. The Mongolian Yuan dynasty demanded tribute from Goryeo, the ally of the defeated Jin dynasty. As for tributes, the Mongol demanded not only special agricultural products but also young women as slaves. When the Goryeo court refused, the Mongols invaded Goryeo numerous times between 1217 and 1258 (Seth 2006:106). After suffering military setbacks, the Goryeo court retreated to Ganghwa island in 1231, while the ordinary Koreans fended for themselves by fighting against Mongol invaders as best as they could. Archery was one of the favored weapon that Koreans used in their fight against the Mongols. In fact, the Mongols withdrew their forces in 1232, after their Mongol commander was killed by an arrow shot by a Korean monk.

Ten years later, in 1233, the Mongols (the Yuan dynasty) invaded Goryeo again and the war continued for several years. Eventually, Yuan and Goryeo agreed to a cease-fire which lasted for six years from 1241 to 1247. Although the members of the royal family were taken to the Yuan Mongolian Empire as hostages, the Goryeo court continued to resist the Mongols. The Yuan dynasty launched more rounds of military attacks between 1247 and 1248. The Mongols killed many Koreans and took over 200,000 as prisoners of war. Historians recorded that wherever the Mongol army passed, "the inhabitants were all burned out" (Seth 2006:107).

Table 2.2 Mongolian Invasions & Mongol's Indirect Rule

1217-1258 (41 years)	The Mongol invasion of Goryeo
1233-1241 (8 years)	The Mongol invasion of Goryeo
1270-1273 (3 years)	The establishment of the pro-Mongol court in Goryeo. The Mongols crushed Goryeo's resistance movement.
1270 -1356 (86 years)	Tributary state to the Mongol Empire (Yuan Dynasty)

The Goryeo court became divided into competing political camps between conciliatory pro-Yuan officials and anti-Yuan hardliners. Eventually, the pro-Mongol faction in the court triumphed. With the help of the Mongols, the throne of Goryeo was passed to a pro-Mongol king in 1270. Meantime, the war continued for three more years, as the anti-Mongol faction in the Goryeo government continued to resist. The anti-Mongol opposition came to an end, after the Mongols crushed Goryeo's last resistance forces on Jindo island in 1271 and Jeju Island in 1273 (Seth 2006).

From 1270 to 1356, Korea remained as a tributary state to the Mongol Empire (the Yuan Dynasty). During this period, Goryeo's crown princes were taken to China's Beijing and stayed there as political hostages. Indicative of their subordinate status to the Yuan dynasty, Goryeo monarchs used the suffix "choong" (meaning "loyal") as the first character of their title as an expression of their loyalty to the Emperor of the Yuan dynasty (Seth 2006: 108). This tradition continued until the reign of King Choongjong (r. 1337-1352) in the mid 14th century. The Goryeo court entered into a marriage alliance with the Yuan dynasty to secure peace. The Goryeo kings, during this period, married princesses of the Yuan royal house as their primary consorts[4]. Starting with Goryeo's king Choong-gyol, Goryeo's royal house continued the tradition of political marriage with princesses of the Yuan dynasty. For instance, King Choongyol (r. 1274-1308) married a daughter of the Yuan emperor Shizu (Seth 2006). For a couple of generations, Goryeo kings followed the practice of marrying princesses of the Yuan imperial house.

K-dramas on the relationship between Goryeo and the Mongolian Empire

As for Goryeo's history during the period of the Mongol's dominance in Asia, three TV series, "King in love", "Empress Ki", and "Faith", depict Goryeo's uneasy relationship with the Mongols (the Yuan Dynasty).

The TV series drama, "King in Love" (or The King loves 왕은 사랑한다), sheds light on the political royal marriage alliance between Goryeo and

---

[4] Marriage for political or diplomatic reasons was also common for centuries among European royal families. The current monarchs of various European countries (England, Spain, the Netherlands, and Denmark) are, by and large, all blood-related since the ruling houses of European kingdoms intermarried over centuries.

the Yuan dynasty by focusing on the life of King Choongseon (r. 1298 and r. 1308-1313), who was the son of a Mongolian prince of the Yuan empire.

Title	The King in Love
Production	Aired in 2017 (40 Episodes)
Cast	Im Si-wan, Im Yoon-ah, Hong Jong-hyun
Synopsis	The drama tells a fictional story of a love triangle involving Crown Prince Won (later King Choongseon) and two fictional figures. It also depicts power struggle in the royal court by shedding light on tension between the Mongolian queen and Goryeo's aristocratic families. (poster © mbc)

The TV series, "Faith", is a fantasy, historical fusion drama, set in the time period of Goryeo in the 14th century. It is a historical fusion drama that mixes the past events with present day life in South Korean society.

Title	Faith
Production	Aired 2012 (24 episodes)
Cast	Lee Min-ho, Kim Hee-sun
Synopsis	This drama tells a fantasy love story between a Goryeo's royal bodyguard and a female doctor from contemporary South Korea. During the reign of King Gongmin (r. 1351-1374), the princess of the Yuan dynasty was fatally injured from an attack by anti-Yuan forces. The head of the royal bodyguard, Choi Young, travels through a mystical time-portal to bring a modern-day doctor who could save the Yuan princess. (poster © sbs)

The TV series, "Empress Ki", tells a fictional love story of Empress Ki. The drama is loosely based on the real historical figure, Empress Ki, a Korean woman who rose to power by marring the last Emperor of the Yuan dynasty, Toghon Temür. As the second wife of the Yuan emperor, Empress Ki exerted a great influence in the Yuan court and Goryeo's, since she had Goryeo's court dominated by pro-Yuan officials including her father and her brothers.

	Title	Empress Ki (기황후)
	Production	2013-2014 (51 Episodes)
	Cast	Ha Ji-won, Ji Chang-wook, Joo Jin-mo
	Synopsis	The main character, Seung Nyang, is a female warrior, pretending to be a man. Hired as a royal guard for a prince of the Yuan dynasty, she becomes the love of two rivals, the King of Goryeo and the Emperor of the Yuan dynasty. (poster © mbc)

The drama, "Empress Ki", provoked a wide-spread criticism for the drama's inaccurate representation of Empress Ki and King Choonghye of Goryeo. Historians point out that the drama distorted Krean history by portraying Empress Ki and King Choonghye as just and patriotic figures. Wang Yoo (the King of Goryeo), a fictional figure in the drama, was portrayed as a brave and caring king, although the real king of Goryeo during that time, King Choonghye (충혜왕), was considered one of the worst kings in Korean history. The producers of the drama claim that the drama is based on a fiction novel and that it is not meant to be a historical documentary. Despite claims about the falsification of Korean history, "Empress Ki" was a commercial success as it became an international hit, the second-highest rated Korean drama after "Jewel in the Palace".

The Fall of Goryeo

In the mid-14th century, the Mongolian rule declined, as Chinese rebellions and uprisings against the Yuan dynasty became more frequent. In 1368, the Chinese rebel forces drove out the Mongols from the capital of China and established the Ming Dynasty instead. Meantime, the territory of the Yuan dynasty was reduced to only a small part of Northern China.

Reflecting the change in balance of power, the Goryeo court became split into two opposing factions, the pro-Yuan versus the pro-Ming. Taking advantage of Yuan's weakness, King Gongmin (공민왕 r. 1351 – 1374) eliminated the pro-Mongol faction in the Goryeo court in 1356[5]. King Gongmin, dropped the suffix "choong (loyal)" from his title and thereby abolished the pro-Yuan tradition. While King Gongmin pursued a pro-Ming policy, the Goryeo court saw fierce rivalry between pro-Ming and pro-Yuan factions (Pratt and Rutt 1999: 244). Eventually, the pro-Yuan faction assassinated King Gongmin and took power in the court.

K-drama on Goryeo during the post-Yuan period		
The drama, "Shin Don", is based on some historical events during the reign of King Gongmin (r. 1351-1374).		

	Title	Sin Don
	Aired	2005-2006 (61 episodes)
	Cast	Son Chang-min
	Synopsis	This drama tells a story about the relationship between Sin Don, a Buddhist monk, and King Gongmin. It focuses on their reform efforts despite a strong domestic opposition. (poster © MBC)

---

[5] It should be noted that Ki Chol, a brother of Empress Ki (a Korean woman and the second wife of the Mongol Emperor), led the pro-Mongol faction, and that historical events involving the Empress Ki inspired the highly popular but controversial TV series, "Empress Ki", in South Korea.

The progressive King Gongmin appointed a slave monk, Sin Don (1322-1371), as his chief officer. Sin Don advocated radical social reform measures including the emancipation of slaves and land reform favorable to peasants. Together with Sin Don, King Gongmin sought to undermine powerful aristocratic families and strengthen the monarchical power. Consequently, the king came to face a strong opposition from Goryeo's powerful aristocracy. Both Sin Don and King Gongmin were assassinated by their political opponents, so their reform movement ultimately failed (Seth 2006: 111).

After King Gongmin's death, the political division and power rivalry in the court exacerbated. By the end of the 14th century, Goryeo faced both domestic problems and external challenges. Numerous foreign invasions, led by northern tribes from China and Wako pirates from Japan, plagued the country, while Goryeo's aristocratic families were engaged in power rivalry. The political instability, together with widespread corruption in the government, eventually led to the fall of the Goryeo kingdom. As the court was divided over how to deal with the competing dynasties in China as well as with Japanese pirates, Goryeo's court fell into a political disarray. Against this backdrop, General Lee Seong-gye and a group of neo-Confucian scholars overthrew the Goryeo Dynasty. Resisting the pro-Yuan court, the pro-Ming faction led by General Lee Seong-gye waged a coup against the government. General Lee forced King Gongyang to abdicate in 1388 and proclaimed himself a new king. Thereafter, he renamed the country to Joseon (Seth 2006).

The Fall of Goryeo

TV series dealing with the demise of Goryeo are numerous. For instance, they include Shin Don, Jeong Do-jeon, and Six Flying Dragons. Jeong Dojeon is a historical drama that depicts the historical events leading to the downfall of the Goryeo Dynasty and the creation of the Joseon

Dynasty in 1392. It focuses on the chief political strategist, Jeong Dojeon, in the political movement against the pro-Yuan court in Goryeo.

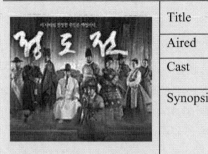

	Title	Jeong Do-jeon
	Aired	in 2014 (50 episodes)
	Cast	Cho Jae-hyun, Yoo Dong-geun
	Synopsis	The drama tells a life story of Jeong Do-jeon. (poster © KBS)

The TV series, "Six Flying Dragons" (육룡이 나르샤), is a well-written political drama that depicts the political situation surrounding the military coup against the last monarch of Goryeo.

	Title	Six Flying Dragons
	Aired	2015 - 2016 (50 Episodes)
	Cast	Yoo Ah-in, Kim Myung-min, Shin Se-kyung, Chun Ho-jin
	Synopsis	The drama focuses on the people who played a crucial role in the coup against the Goryeo dynasty. It sheds light on the ideological and political differences between Lee Bang-won and Jeong Do-jeon, the two main strategists of the creation of Joseon kingdom. (poster © sbs)

Major Historical Figures in the Last Goryeo Court

The following figures are important historical figures who almost always appear in K-dramas and movies depicting the last Goryeo court. To name only a few, they include: Lee Sung-gye, Jeong Mong-ju, Lee Bang-won, and Jeong Do-jeon

Lee Sung-gye (이성계 1335 – 1408) was a Goryeo military general who fought against the Yuan forces in the north and the Japanese pirates in the south. Supporting the pro-Ming faction in the court, he was against waging a war with Ming. He waged a coup against the pro-Yuan government and later founded a new dynasty, called Joseon.

Jeong Mong-ju (1333-1392) was Korea's renowned Neo-Confucian scholar who taught at Sungkyungwan, the highest academic institution of Goryeo. Being loyal to the Goryeo dynasty, he opposed Lee's plan to overthrow the government. He was later assassinated by Lee's son, Lee Bang-won (Han 1995).

Lee Bang-won (이방원 1367 – 1492) was the 5th son of Lee Sung-gye. He played an important role in supporting his father Lee Sung-gye and the pro-Ming faction in the court. Later, he became the third king of Joseon, King Taejong. Before the coup against Goryeo, Lee Bang-won sought to win Jeong Mong-ju to his side. He composed the following poem to win Jeong over to his sides.

> This won't matter, that won't matter.
> It won't matter if the vines at Mt. Mansu get interlaced.
> Let us mingle together like this and enjoy it for a hundred years.

But Jeong Mong-ju, being loyal to the Goryeo's monarch, refused to take part in the coup. He answered Lee Bang-won with the following poem, titled "Danshim-ga (The Song of Steadfast Heart),".

> This body may die a hundred deaths
> And my white bones may turn to dust and my soul may cease to exist
> But my steadfast heart for my beloved will never die.

"My beloved" in Jeong's poem referred to his unwavering loyalty to his sovereign, the king of Goryeo. The two famous poems are available in most Korean school history books. All Korean students, who get tested for their knowledge of Korean history relating to the transition from Goryeo and Joseon, must know the two poems.

Like Jeong Mong-ju, Jeong Do-jeon (1342-1398) was also a renowned neo-Confucian scholar and a member of the faculty at Sungkyungwan. Due to his opposition to the pro-Yuan faction in the court, he was exiled for almost 10 years. Later, he joined forces with Lee Sung-gye and acted as Lee's chief political adviser. Highly critical of Buddhism and Taoism, he developed a political philosophy based on Neo-Confucian ideas. He called for people-oriented progressive policies including land and tax reform favorable to peasants. Jeong Dojeon, a prolific writer, produced many works on politics. He advocated the cabinet-centered government with the nominal rule of the king, whereby a prime minister is in real charge of the duties of administration. While serving as the first Prime Minister of Joseon, he helped to shape the constitutional character of Joseon's governance system by authoring Joseon's first code of laws, called "Joseon Gyeong-guk-jeon". Although he rose to the position of the prime minister, he was later assassinated by Lee Bang-won due to their political differences (Oliver 1993).

Chapter 3

Joseon Kingdom (1392-1910)

Socio-Political Changes

In 1392, General Lee founded the Joseon dynasty and moved the capital from Gaesung to Hanyang (present-day Seoul) (KOCIS 2019). The new dynasty introduced a series of policies that transformed the socio-political character of the society.

The socio-political changes included:

- The founding political philosophy of the state: Neo-Confucianism
- Demotion of Buddhism
- Land reform
- Centralization of monarchical power
- Restriction on slavery
- Expansion of educational institutions and civil service exams
- Decline of women's status

Several changes by the Joseon dynasty stand out. The first change was the adoption of neo-Confucianism as the state's ruling ideology, as opposed to Goryeo's state-sponsored Buddhism. The Joseon dynasty took measures to eliminate Buddhist interferences in government affairs, while elevating neo-Confucianism to the founding political philosophy of the Joseon court. One of the main founders of Joseon, Jeong Do-jeon, was very critical of Buddhist monks' involvement in politics and government's heavy expenditure for supporting temples and elaborate Buddhist rituals. The new dynasty, under the political influence of the neo-Confucian scholar Jeong Do-jeon, took measures to end the collusive relationship between Buddhist institutions and the state by prohibiting state-sponsorship of Buddhism. For instance, Buddhist temples lost their privileges such as tax exemptions (Seth 2006: 123). In addition, the new king confiscated some holdings of Buddhist temples and redistributed them to his supporters as taxable properties. With Buddhist temples cut off from official patronage, Buddhism saw a relative decline in Joseon. Yet despite the predominantly anti-Buddhist sentiment of the Neo-Confucians in the state, Buddhism remained as a folk religion and continued to play an important role in the lives of ordinary Korean people.

The second important change is the land reform, albeit very modest. Initially, the Neo-Confucianist Jeong Do-jeon, one of the founders of the Joseon dynasty, pushed for radical land reform that would convert all land into public property which would then be equally redistributed among all the peasants. Jeong emphasized the Confucian idea that the ruler must govern in the interests of the welfare of his people. To pacify the opposition from large landowning yangbans, the Joseon court, however, opted for a mild and selective form of land reform by confiscating only the estates of some aristocratic families and Buddhist temples (Han 1995). An anti-Buddhist land reform was also beneficial to the new government that needed to bring more land under government taxation to expand state revenues (Seth 2006:123). By and large, the privileged position of the aristocratic families (yangban) did not fundamentally change under the new regime. Most Goryeo officials continued to serve for the Joseon court since the coup purged only a small number of top officials in the government (Seth 2006).

The third change was the introduction of state regulations on the use of slaves. For the new government, too many private slaves were a problem since it meant fewer taxpaying peasants and fewer commoners to serve in the military. Although all slaves were exempted from compulsory military service, public slaves were an important source of government income and a cheap labor force for the construction of public buildings and infrastructures (Seth 2006). Thus, Joseon's founder, Lee Sung-gye, converted 80,000 slaves of Buddhist temples to public slaves for the state. Historians note that public slaves, belonging to the state, numbered around 350,000 in the late 15th century (Seth 2006: 162).

The fourth change is the centralization of power, albeit limited. In 1413, King Taejong (r. 1400-1418) established the "hopae" identification system that recorded census data, tax collection, migration and runaway slaves (Seth

2006:144). King Taejong further strengthened monarchical power by abolishing private armies and by keeping only armed forces under the government. With the creation of the central army, the era of private armies of the aristocracy came to an end and only the central state had the monopoly on armed forces (Seth 2006:136).

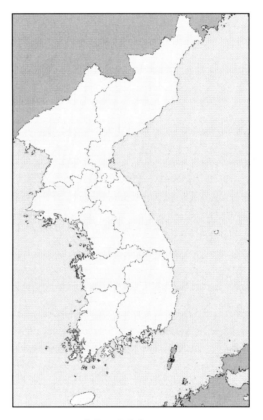

Map 3.1 Joseon

The fifth change is the decline of women's social status due to neo-Confucianism, the founding philosophy of Joseon. Neo-Confucianism is a male-centered philosophy that preached the subordination of women to men as part of the natural order of society. In Joseon, women could no longer freely interact with men at public social gatherings. It became customary for women to wear veils in public places. Women had to seek the permission of husbands or family heads before participating in social activities. Horse riding, a common activity among upper-class Goryeo women, was forbidden by law in 1402. Widows were no longer allowed to remarry. Married women were required to have their long-braided hair coiled and held together with a long pin, called "binyo". Although women still could inherit property until the 17th century, households headed by women gradually disappeared in Joseon (Seth 2006: 155 & 157).

The System of Governance in Joseon

Gyeongguk daejeon, Joseon's founding constitution, outlines the basic laws relating to the governance system of Joseon. Since historical dramas on Joseon almost always contain references to various ministries and other governmental bodies, it is useful to get some basic information about the political system of the Joseon dynasty. The summary of Joseon's governing system is provided in the table below.

Table 3.1 The System of governance in Joseon (source: Seth 2006)

Eujeongbu (State Council 의정부)	The state council supervised all government offices and affairs. Most State Council members were selected through the civil service examination, while the three highest-ranking members, the High State Councillors, were appointed by the king (Seth 2006: 125).
	Ijo (Ministry of Personnel 이조) supervised the procedures of recruiting personnel, including nominations for office, certification of appointments, ranks, titles, and evaluation of the performance of office holders.
	Hojo (Ministry of Revenue 호조) supervised the collection of taxes, maintaining population registers, conducting land surveys and land registers, and distributing funds. This ministry had several committees specializing in the following areas: • Naeja-si (palace foodstuff and weaving necessities) • Naesom-si (palace wine/entertainment of foreign envoys) • Sajae-gam (meat, fish, salt, firewood and charcoal) • Gunja-gam (Military supplies) • Pyonsi-so (market prices, weights and measures) • Yanghyon-go (food for Sungkyungwan students and faculty)

Yukjo (Six Ministries 육조)	Yejo (Ministry of Rites 예조) supervised state ceremonies, the schools and examinations, licensed monks. The ministry supervised the following organizations: Sungkyungwan (National University), Chunchu-gwan (State archive), Sungmun-won (diplomatic correspondence), Sayog-won (Office of translators), Sahak (the four colleges of Seoul), Chonui-gam (Distribution of medicines), Hyemin-so (medical relief for the people), Naeui-won (preparing medicaments), Binggo (ice-houses), Gwansang-gam (Astronomical and meteorological observation and records; calendar; water-clocks), Dohwa-seo (Painting). In addition, the Ministry of Rites had special institutions dealing with banquets for guests, royal relations and officers of 1st and 2nd grades.
	Byongjo (Ministry of War 병조) supervised various organizations for military training, horses and stables, weapon production, fortification, post roads, beacon fire communication systems, and the guards of the Crown Prince.
	Hyungjo (Ministry of Punishment 형조) dealt with investigating and prosecuting civil and criminal cases as well as sentencing. While magistrates handle most criminal cases, the Eugeumboo (State Tribunal) was at the top of the judicial system. The ministry of Punishment also dealt with registering and freeing of slaves and prisoners.
	Kongjo (Ministry of Public Work 공조) supervised various organizations for construction and repair of public buildings (such as palace and parks), roads, state mining and lumbering operations, and the production of articles for state use by the corps of state artisans including paper making. (Pratt and Rutt 1999: 150-151)
Central Government censorate	Uigeum-bu (Royal inquisition 의금부) Sahon-bu (Government censorate 사헌부) Sungjong-won (Receipt and issue of decrees 성종원) Sagan-won (Royal censorate 사간원) Kyongwon (Royal lectures)
Royal Councils	Jongchin-bu dealt with royal family affairs. Choonghun-bu dealt with the affairs of meritorious subjects. Uibin-bu dealt with the affairs of Royal Sons-in Law. Tolryong-bu dealt with the affairs of royal relations by blood and marriage. Pongo-ha dealt with ceremonial duties of noble pensioners.

After the monarch, the highest body of power in the government was the Eujeongbu (State Council) which consisted of seven members. The day-to-day administration was carried out by the Yukjo (Six Ministries) that governed affairs relating to taxation, military affairs, punishments, and public works, among others. Each ministry was headed by a board consisting of three or four ministers. As shown in table 3.1, the system of governance in Joseon remained more or less unchanged for about 500 years (Seth 2006:125-126).

K-dramas on Joseon's system of governance

The TV series, "Daejang-geum: Jewel in the Palace", sheds light on the workings of Joseon's governance system including various ministries and governmental bodies.

	Title	Daejang-geum: Jewel in the Palace
	Production	Aired in 2003 (51 episodes)
	Cast	Lee Young-Ae, Ji Jin-Hee
	Synopsis	The drama is based on the true story of Jang Geum, who became Joseon's first female royal physician. Despite opposition in the court, she became a royal chef and then later a royal physician. The drama follows various court intrigues against her. (Poster © MBC)

The drama achieved global popularity in over 90 countries around the world and was exported to numerous countries.

Gwageo (State Examination, 과거)

The government offices were staffed by the successful candidates who passed a series of state examination, called "gwageo (과거)". The gwageo system, first introduced from China to Unified Silla in 788, further expanded and was perfected during the early period of Joseon, and continued to be the main method of appointment until the end of 19th century (Cho, WJ 2000: 687). The Ministry of Personnel (Ijo) supervised the staffing of the state bureaucracy with people who passed the state examinations with excellent scores. Gwageo was divided into three types: moogwa (military service exam), moongwa (civil service exam), and japgwa (technical service exam).

Moo-gwa (military service exam 무과): Moogwa was the military examination for the recruitment of military personnel. It tested the candidate's skills in martial arts (lancing, archery, horse-riding) and knowledge of the Five Classics and the Seven Military Classics (Han 1995). Initially, only 28 finalists were selected every year but from King Injo's reign (r. 1626-1649) onward, the number of the recruited increased to several hundreds or even thousands (Cho, WJ 2000: 690).

Jap-gwa (technical service exam 잡과): Through the japgwa exam, the government certified the nation's specialists in astrology, medicine, law, geography and foreign language (Mandarin, Japanese, Mongolian and Manchu) (Pratt and Rutt 1999: 115). Successful candidates of japgwa were appointed to various technical posts in the government as doctors, interpreters, painters, and astronomers. Annually, 10 professionals were selected for each field including medicine, law, and geography (Cho, WJ 2000: 690-691).

Moon-gwa (civil service exam 문과): Moongwa was the most prestigious exam of the three types. The civil exam tested the candidate's knowledge of the Four Books and Five Classics of Confucianism[6]. It also tested candidate's skills in composing poetry and essays on any given topic (Han 1995; Cho, WJ 2000). The moongwa exam has three stages. The first stage was a preliminary provincial level exam which issued the lower degree (saengwon or chinsa degree) to successful candidates. A total of 1400 scholars were annually selected nationwide. They were given lower level administrative posts in the government or admission to study at the prestigious Sungkyungwan university. The second stage was the metropolitan exam in Seoul, the capital of Joseon. Only the candidates who passed the first stage became eligible for the advanced level exam. About 200 or 100 were chosen

---

[6] The Four Books and Five Classics refers to the written collection and compilation of speeches by Confucius and Mencius as well as the commentaries by Confucian scholars. The Four Books are: The Great Learning, The Doctrine of the Mean, Confucian Analects and The Works of Mencius. The Five Classics are: The Book of Poetry, The Book of History, The Book of Rites, The Book of Changes, and The Spring and Autumn Annals.

and given the respective degree. They were appointed to the middle level administrative posts in the government (Cho, WJ 2000: 687). The third stage was the cheonsi (palace exam 천시), which took place under the supervision of the king, and was available only for the top thirty-three examinees who succeeded in the second stage (Seth 2006:130). The successful candidates of the palace exam were individually ranked and appointed to high-level government posts.

Neo-Confucianism emphasizes meritocracy whereby society is governed by people of knowledge, skills and virtue. Following the neo-Confucian teaching, the early Joseon court gave greater importance to the recruitment of government officials through the gwageo system. The government expanded educational opportunities to the broader populace including the commoners (Seth 2006).

While some commoners indeed took advantage of the civil exams to advance their social status, they remained a minority and almost always failed to reach the top-tier civil exam. The highest level of moongwa exam functioned mainly as the selection device for the yangban class. Formal equality before the law rarely translated into an actual opportunity for the peasantry and other classes, since the commoners could not afford to take time off from strenuous farm work for lengthy studies at provincial or capital colleges in far-away places. Since formal education was largely organized around preparation for the gwageo exams, one had to be away from village to attend schools at all levels from seodang (elementary schools in their own or nearby village) to Sungkyungwan (the national state university) or hyanggyo (provincial colleges).

Joseon's Educational System

The system of staffing state bureaucracy relied on Joseon's education system that prepared people for civil service examinations. Six types of educational institutions existed in Joseon. They include: the national college (Sungkyungwan), capital colleges (sahak), provincial colleges (hyanggyo), vocational schools (shiphak), primary schools (seodang), and private colleges (seowon). All educational institutions were exempted from paying government taxes and received subsidies such as free land. With the exception of some private schools (e.g., seowon), the government fully financed educational institutions at all levels. The Ministry of Rites (Yejo) managed all schools with the minutely stipulated regulations that required all schools to adhere to laws concerning the use of textbooks, class attendance, monthly and annual tests, seating capacity, reward and penalty (Cho, WJ 2000: 687).

Table 3.2 Educational System of Joseon

---

1. Primary schools (seodang)
2. Vocational schools (shiphak)
3. Provincial colleges (Hyanggyo)
4. Capital Colleges (Sahak)
5. Private Colleges (Seowon)
6. National college (Sungkyungwan)

---

* Seodang (서당): Primary Schools

Seodang is the equivalent to a primary school. Available in most villages throughout the country, seodang is free and open to everyone except the lower classes and women. For the commoners, schooling was limited to seodang elementary school. Women of the aristocratic yangban class were educated by private tutors at home (Seth 2006: 134).

* Shiphak (십학): Vocational schools

Shiphak is equivalent to a vocational school. Mostly members of the Joongin class (technicians and artisans) attended vocational schools (shiphak). Vocational schools trained students in the following subjects: arithmetics, law, medicine, language, astronomy, geography, painting, and music. Joseon had two schools of medicine and a school of law which taught mainly criminal law and trial procedure. The size of enrollment was strictly regulated. The school of medicine had about 3,440 enrollments, while the enrollment for the school of law was capped at about 3,400. The language schools taught Chinese, Mongolian, Jurchen (Manchu), and Japanese language (Cho, WJ 2000: 686).

* Hyanggyo (향교) and Sahak (사학): Provincial and Capital Colleges

Hyanggyo (provincial colleges) and Sahak (capital colleges) are equivalent to present-day colleges. Although these colleges were open to everybody (from 15 years or older) from all classes, the overwhelming number of students came from the yangban class. Joseon had more than 300 provincial colleges throughout the country and 4 capital colleges (sahak) in Seoul. According to the government regulation concerning enrollment, a provincial college could accept only 30-50 students annually, while a capital colleges (sahak) could take up to 100 students. Hyanggyo students with good academic standing could also enter Sungkyungwan or take the state examination for lower degrees. College students were exempted from military duty during the duration of their studies (Cho, WJ 2000).

* Sungkyungwan (성균관)

Established in 1398, Sungkyungwan (SKG) was the highest learning institution of Joseon, equivalent to a national university. Completely financed by the government, SKG had the student enrollment capped at around 200 and had a teaching and administrative staff of 30-40 officials. Given that only those who passed the lower level exams could be admitted, SKG attracted only the students with highest academic standing (Joe, WJ 2000: 675). SKG students had some privileges including access to various literary and military (mainly archery) events that took place in the royal presence.

SKG students had an autonomous student council, a body of student representatives. The Student Council was the self-government of students that had the power to discipline its members and to critique even the royal court (Joe, WJ 2000: 676). At times, the Student Council organized students' opposition in the form of "yuso" (a protest letter). Yuso is an official protest letter of the student collective given to the royal court when students and scholars sought to change some aspects of government policies. In addition to Yuso, the protestors often wage a sit-down strike in front of the royal palace. It was recorded that one of students' longest strikes was against the government's educational policy in 1551 and that the strike lasted for 6 months. During the 18th century, student strikes were most frequent. During the reign of king Yongjo (r. 1725-1776), students went on strike 18 times, while 16 strikes occurred under the reign of king Chongjo (r. 1777-1800) (Joe, WJ 2000: 677).

K-drama on Joseon's Education System

As for K-dramas that depict Joseon's educational system, the TV series, "Sungkyungwan Scandal" (성균관 스캔들), is a must-see. With the focus on the life of students and faculty members at Sungkyungwan, Joseon's highest education institution, the drama shed light on gwageo, the system of civil service exams, and the rampant political factionalism among the elite in the Joseon society.

Title	Sungkyungwan Scandal
Episode	Aired in 2010 (20 episodes)
Cast	Park Min-young, Park Yoo-cheon
Synopsis	Set in the time of King Jeongjo's reign (r.1776-1800), the drama depicts student life at Sungkyunkwan university. It focuses on Kim Yoon-hee who disguised herself as a boy to study at Sungkyungwan. Three male students, despite different political lineages, all come to care for Kim without knowing her true identity. (Poster © KBS)

The drama, "Sungkyungwan Scandal", sheds light on political factionalism rampant in the 18th century Joseon. For details about the political factionalism, please read the relevant section at the end of this chapter.

* Chongsa (청사) and Seowon (서원): Private schools and others academic institutions:

Private academies such as "seowon" and "chongsa" existed as alternatives to state-sponsored schools and colleges such as hyanggyo or sahak (Cho, WJ 2000: 696-7). In late Joseon, some scholars critical of rigid and outdated Confucianism, advocated a "silhak" (practical learning) philosophy that emphasized the learning of scientific and practical knowledge. Against this background, they established private schools as alternatives to the state-run schools. By the end of the 19th century, private academies in Joseon numbered around 680 (Cho, WJ 2000: 703).

Social Stratification

Joseon had four distinctive social classes: the yangban (the aristocracy), the joong-in (the professional middle class), the pyeongmin (the commoners) and the cheonmin (the lower class). Legally speaking, the class distinction was not hereditary since the law did not prohibit the commoners and the middle-class people (the joongin) from becoming members of the yangban group. In theory, social mobility was possible mainly through the venues of state exams (gwageo). Everyone except the cheonmin class had the right to attend schools, take state exams, and serve in government office (Seth 2006: 159). In reality, however, economic disparity seriously limited social mobility.

- Yangban (양반)

The term "yangban" refers to people who belonged to the group of neo-Confucian scholars and high-rank government officials, and their family members. The yangban, literally meaning "two sides" in Korean, consists of two types of government officials, moon-ban (civil officials) and moo-ban (military officials) (Seth 2006: 126-127). They enjoyed many privileges such as tax exemption. In comparison to the moonban (civil officials), the moo-ban (military officials) held relatively lower social esteem due to neo-Confucian focus on literature and arts (Han 1995). Although most yangbans owned land, landownership was not the main criterion that differentiated the yangban from the rest of the other classes. Some rich farmers and professionals from the "joongin" class could also own land. In this regard, it should be also noted that since neo-Confucianism disdained for commerce, the yangban class was prohibited from engaging in commercial activities. Commerce was relegated to only the commoners and the middle-class joongin.

- Joong-in (the middle Class 중인)

The Joongin (literally meaning "middlemen" in Korean) refers to technical specialists who hold low-to-middle rank positions in the government. They include clerks, astrologers, doctors, interpreters, accountants, and legal professionals. To become a member of the joongin class, people must obtain a government issued certificate after they successfully pass the specialized "japgwa" exam (Seth 2006: 163). Since neo-Confucians detested technical knowledge and commerce, the joongin held the lower social status in comparison to the yangban.

- Pyeongmin (the commoners 평민)

The pyeongmin (the commoners) included independent farmers, tenant farmers, artisans, shop keepers and merchants. The commoners had to pay taxes and to shoulder the burden of corvée (public works).

- Cheonmin (the lower class 천민)

Public and private slaves and members of the outcaste groups belonged to the cheonmin (the lower class) group. The outcast groups included innkeepers, ferrymen, entertainers, butchers, and shamans (Seth 2006: 163). Unlike all other classes, the cheonmin was a truly hereditary class, since no legal venue for social mobility was available to them.

As for slaves, about 200,000 slaves were estimated to have had existed in Joseon in the mid-17th century (Pratt, and Rutt 1999:429). Some governmental efforts were made to abolish slavery. Starting with the destruction of all records of slave status within the royal household, official slavery was abolished in 1801 with a few exceptions. Although the number of public slaves significantly declined, private slaves (resident slavery) did not disappear. Although the government abolished all hereditary forms of slavery in 1886, it took 10 more years until all forms of slavery including private ones completely disappeared (Pratt, and Rutt 1999; Seth 2006).

Slaves in Joseon

The TV series drama, "The Slave Hunters" (추노), shed light on Joseon's slavery system in the 17th century.

Title	The Slave Hunters
Year	2010 (24 episodes)
cast	Jang Hyuk
Synopsis	Set in the time of King Injo's reign (r. 1623-1649), the drama tells a story about a slave hunter and a run-away slave woman (Poster © KBS).

Professional female entertainers, known as giesaeng, frequently appear in historical dramas and films. By performing music and dance, they entertain their male patrons at private and public banquets (Pratt and Rutt 1999). Giesaengs belonged to a special category within the cheonmin class. Giesaengs were given a special treatment and even enjoyed some privileges. They were taught reading, calligraphy, music, dance and other liberal arts, while some courtesans were trained in martial arts such as horsemanship, archery or sword-play (Han 1995).

Giesaeng in Joseon

Hwang Jin-yi, a TV series, is based on the real story of Hwang Jin-yi (1506- 1546) who was a giesaeng and a famous poet in the 16th century.

Title	Hwang Jin-yi (황진이)
Year	Aired in 2006 (24 episodes)
Cast	Ha Ji-won as Hwang Jin-yi
Synopsis	Born to a low-class mother, Hwang Jin-yi has limited opportunities despite her brilliant artistic talents. She falls in love with a young man from a noble family. As the class division prohibits their love, she makes a decision that will change her life forever. (Poster © KBS)

Hwang Jin-yi's poems are famous for verses of beautiful landscapes, love, and longing. Hwang Jin-yi was admired by many of Joseon's scholars for her intelligence and artistic talent. Several TV series, films, and novels have been made to celebrate her work.

Joseon's Arts, Literature, and Scientific Achievements

The greatest cultural achievement of all, during the period of the Joseon dynasty, is the invention of the Korean Alphabet, Hangeul. Until the 15th century, the Korean people used only Chinese characters as the main means of written communication. King Sejong (r.1418-1450), the fourth King of Joseon, wanted to create a simple writing script system based on phonetic principles, so that the commoners, illiterate farmers and women could easily learn and use the easier script instead of the complex Chinese ideograms. With the help of a few trusted scholars, King Sejong secretly invented "Hangeul", the phonetic Korean writing script[7], in 1443. Despite a strong opposition from the ruling elite in the royal court and neo-Confucian scholars, the king fostered the use of Hangeul among the populace by publicly disseminating the new script in 1446.

K-drama on Hangeul, the Korean Writing Script

Since King Sejong the Great is regarded as the greatest king in Korean history, it is no surprise then that more than a dozen TV series and films have been made to celebrate his achievements.

The TV series, "Trees with deep roots", is based on the real story of King Sejong the Great who fought against the neo-Confucian establishment that

---

[7] Hangeul was not based on any existent writing scripts. King Sejong invented Korean consonants resembling the shape of vocal cord and embouchure. For example, ㄱ, the first consonant in Hangeul is based on the shape the tongue makes when making the ㄱ sound.

opposed the creation of Hangeul, the Korean alphabet system, and the King's efforts to make it available to the general populace.

Title	Deep Rooted Tree (Tree with Deep Roots)
Year	Aired in 2011 (24 episodes)
Cast	Han Suk-ku, Jang Hyuk, Shin Se-kyung
Synopsis	This drama depicts court intrigues against King Sejong and his endeavor to create the Korean alphabet. King Sejong tries to stop political forces against the invention of Hangeul that was ultimately designed to empower the commoners. (Poster © SBS)

The film, "Naramalssami (나라말싸미)", also depicts King Sejong's endeavour to create the Korean script, Hangeul. Compared to the TV drama, "Deep Rooted Tree", the film focuses on the role of the Queen and a Buddhist monk in helping King Sejong with the invention of Hangeul.

During the reign of King Sejong, Korean arts and science flourished. King Sejong sponsored scientific scholarship and cultural work. He set up the jiphyeonjeon, a national research institute, and a royal observatory. Many scientific inventions were made during his reign. Great advancements were made in astronomy, medicine, irrigation methods, national defense, and printing technology, as well as music. The observatory measured the exact altitude of the sun and helped Joseon's scientists to construct eighteen astronomical instruments and a star map (Pratt, and Rutt 1999:409). Under the aegis of King Sejong, Jang Yon-sil (a former slave who became a renowned scientist) invented numerous devices such as astronomical clocks, water clocks, and sundials. King Sejong fostered the dissemination of scientific and practical knowledge to the populace (Seth 2006:144).

Joseon's Scientific Achievements and Jang Yon-sil

The TV series, "Jang Yeong-sil", follows the life story of Jang Yeong-sil, one of the greatest scientists and inventors during the early period of the Joseon dynasty.

	Title	Jang Yeong-sil
	Year	Aired in 2016 (24 Episodes)
	cast	Song Il-gook, Kim Yeong-chul
	Synopsis	Jang Yeong-sil was a genius man with keen interests in astronomy but had no opportunities to realize his potentials since he was born as a slave. Despite many obstacles, his scientific inventions caught the attention of some government officials close to King Sejong. (Poster © KBS)

The drama also sheds light on King Sejong's endeavour to foster scientific development. Although Jang Yeong Sil was born as a slave, King Sejong allowed him to carry out scientific work under his protection. Jang invented numerous devices including astronomical instruments, an iron printing press and a water clock.

With the promulgation of Hangeul, the level of literacy among women and the commoners drastically improved. Confucian scholars and the aristocratic class adamantly opposed the use of Hangeul even after its promulgation. In fact, Hangeul was not used in official publications until the end of the Joseon period. Official publications, scholarship, and the literary work by yangban was written in Chinese. In contrast, the commoners and women mostly used Hangeul as the main vehicle for written communication and informal writing. Gradually, however, Hangeul was spread to the populace and it became widely used in popular literature (Seth 2006: 173).

Thanks to the Korean Alphabet and the improved printing technology, the post-Sejong generations saw a rapid proliferation of popular literature written in Korean. Hundreds of fictions, the majority of which was written by anonymous authors, became widely circulated and read among the people of all classes. Examples of the popular folks' literature, written in Korean, included: The Tale of Hong Gil-dong, Choonhyangjeon, and Simcheongjeon. One of the widely read Korean novels in the 16th century was the story of Hong Gildong, a Korean version of the Robin Hood story. In addition, a large body of women's literature emerged in the era of Hangeul. For instance, court ladies wrote many stories about the intrigues of the royal court, which was known as the palace literature.

Joseon's Folk Literature

Some historical fusion dramas are based on folktales and legendary figures of the folk literature produced during the Joseon period. They include: The Legend of the Blue Sea, Gu Family Book, Hong Gil-dong, and Arang and the Magistrate, among many others.

The TV series, "Hong Gil-dong", draws on a legendary figure from Korean folk literature. Written by Heo Gyun (1569–1618), "The Tale of Hong Gildong", tells the story about Hong Gildong, the child of a nobleman and a female servant. Although he is a very intelligent man, he experiences many forms of discrimination because of his social status as an illegitimate son. The Joseon society did not allow illegitimate sons to take the civil service exam, the main venue for occupational opportunities and social mobility. Eventually, he runs away from his home. After learning martial arts and swordplay, he organizes a group of society's outcasts including thieves. His group robs only the corrupt politicians and the rich who amassed wealth by unjust means. He and his band of thieves redistribute the wealth to the poor. The novel ends with a happy ending, whereby he and his followers move to a foreign place called Yuldo and establish an ideal society based on equality and justice.

In reality, however, the opposite outcome waited for the author and like-minded people in the 17th century Joseon. For the novel disseminates a revolutionary idea of overthrowing the existing social hierarchy, the author was charged with a treason of conspiring an uprising against the monarchy and was executed in 1618 (Seth 2006: 176).

	Title	Fast Sword Hong Gil-dong
	Production	Aired in 2008 (24 episodes)
	Cast	Gang Ji-hwan, Sung Yu-ri, Jang Geun-suk
	Synopsis	While drawing on Heo Gyun's novel, "The Tale of Hong Gildong", the TV drama adds lots of new stories that result in a very different ending compared to the original in the novel. (poster © KBS)

Set in the time period of King Seonjo's reign (r.1567-1608), the TV series, "The Legend of the Blue Sea", creatively draws on a legendary figure from the Korean folk literature, "Sim Cheong", and Andersen's' classic fairy tale of the little mermaid. In the folk tale, Sim Cheong is a pious daughter who sacrifices herself to save her blind father. She plunges into the sea as a maiden sacrifice for fishermen who try to appease Okhwansangje, the King of the Sea.

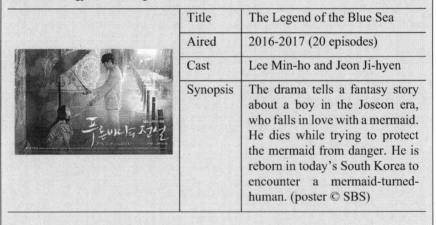

	Title	The Legend of the Blue Sea
	Aired	2016-2017 (20 episodes)
	Cast	Lee Min-ho and Jeon Ji-hyen
	Synopsis	The drama tells a fantasy story about a boy in the Joseon era, who falls in love with a mermaid. He dies while trying to protect the mermaid from danger. He is reborn in today's South Korea to encounter a mermaid-turned-human. (poster © SBS)

The TV series, "Gu Family Book", is a historical fantasy drama, based on Korean folklores about "gumiho", a half human and half fox with nine tails. More than a dozen of TV series and films are based on the gumiho related folktales.

	Title	Book of the House of Gu (구가의 서)
	Production	Aired in 2003 (24 episodes)
	Cast	Lee Seung-gi, Bae Suzy
	Synopsis	The drama tells a story about a gumiho (a half human and half beast) who falls in love with a human. In order to become a human, the gumiho must refrain from doing certain things for 100 days. (poster © MBC)

Other literature genres such as poetry flourished during the Joseon period. Since the gwageo (the civil exam) emphasizes people's skill to compose verses and poetry, Sijo (the poetry in Chinese style) thrived in Confucian Joseon. In a parallel development, many Koreans including yangban women and giesaeng composed verses in Korean. Some of the greatest poets in the mid 16th century Joseon include Yun Son-do (1587-1671) and Hwang Jin-yi (1506-1544) (Seth 2006).

The Joseon dynasty saw also the emergence of many great painters including Kim Hong-do and Sin Yun-bok. Including Kim and Sin, many of Joseon's famous painters were trained at Dohwaso, the Academy of Fine Arts under the supervision of the Ministry of Rites. Dohwaso was a state-sponsored institution for training professional painters. Kim Hong-do (1745-1818) is famous for his paintings of ordinary farmers and artisans working in their fields or their shops. Sin Yun-bok (1758-?) is famous for his realistic paintings of daily life involving giesaeng (female entertainer) and yangban. Due to conservative Neo-Confucian disapproval, Sin was expelled from Dohwaso, but he is today remembered as one of the great Joseon artists (Seth 2006: 198)

TV dramas on Joseon's arts

The TV series, "Painter of the Wind", sheds light on Joseon's painters at Dohwaseo. The drama presents a fictional story about Shin Yun-bok and Kim Hong-do, the two great painters of the Joseon kingdom.

	Title	Painter of the Wind (바람의 화원)
	Year	Aired in 2006 (24 episodes)
	Cast	Moon Geun-yeong, Park Sin-yang
	Synopsis	In real life, Shin Yun-bok was a man but the drama fictionalized the painter as a woman. She pretends to be a boy and studies at Dohwaseo, the royal institute for training painters. She encounters Kim Hong-do, a master painter of Joseon at that time. (Poster © SBS)

The TV series drama, "Saimdang: Memoir of Colors," is a fantasy fiction drama that sheds light on the life of Saimdang (1504-1551), a famous female artist in the 16th century Joseon.

	Title	Saimdang: Memoir of Colors (사임당: 빛의 일기)
	Production	Aired in 2017 (28 episodes)
	Cast	Lee Yong-ae and Song Seung-heon
	Synopsis	A university lecturer discovers an old diary of Saimdang, a famous artist from the 16th century Joseon. The diary reveals Saimdang's life stories including numerous political challenges that she faced as a female artist in the conservative Joseon society (poster © SBS).

Inter-state Relations in East Asia and Foreign Invasions

Starting from the reign of King Sejong the Great (r.1418-1450), Joseon enjoyed a period of peace and cultural renaissance for more than two hundred years. King Sejong greatly enhanced Korea's national security by improving military technology and strengthening Joseon's frontiers. To consolidate Joseon's border, he enforced the settlement of Koreans in the previously scarcely populated areas near the borders. He also used the policies of military campaigns and the construction of forts to enhance national security. As a result, King Sejong was able to firmly establish the borders of Korea that have not changed much to the present day (Seth 2006: 138).

The relatively peaceful period of Joseon, however, came to an end by the end of the 16th century. Joseon experienced two major foreign invasions between the late 16th and the early 17th century. The first invasion was by the Japanese and the second one by the Manchurians.

Imjinwaeran (1592-1598): The Japanese Invasions

In 1592, Japan under the powerful warlord Hideyoshi invaded Joseon with a quarter of a million men. Known as Imjinwaeran (meaning "the incident in imjin years" in Korean), it was recorded as one of the largest overseas invasions in Asian history before the 20th century (Seth 2006:140). Unaware of the seriousness of Japan's military campaigns, the Joseon court was utterly unprepared for Japan's surprise attack. Three weeks after the invasion, the Japanese captured Joseon's capital and then pushed further north. King Seonjo (r. 1567-1608) fled to Uiju near the border to China and asked the Ming dynasty for help. Meantime, the Korean masses were left to fend for themselves. Koreans from all walks of life including the commoners, slaves, monks and some yangbans, organized themselves into an unofficial army of civilians, called "eubyeong" (the Righteous Army), and fought against the Japanese invaders.

The Ming dynasty, responding to Joseon's call for help, entered the war in January 1593. The Ming-Joseon allied forces, together with the Korean militia, the Righteous Army (eubyeong), drove away the Japanese from

Pyeongyang (Seth 2006:140). Meanwhile, Korean naval forces under the leadership of Admiral Lee Soon-sin (1545-1598) destroyed hundreds of Japanese ships. As the Joseon-Ming joint forces pushed back the Japanese and confined battles to the southern coastal region, the war went into a stalemate by 1594. In the meanwhile, Japan tried to strike a bargain with China's Ming dynasty. Japan's Hideyoshi offered China a deal that would divide Korea, with the southern half under Japanese control, while allowing China to control the northern part of Joseon (Pratt, and Rutt, 1999:184). Refusing Japan's proposal, the Ming dynasty instead offered Japan to become part of the Chinese tributary system. As Sino-Japanese negotiations broke down, Japan mobilized 141,500 troops to attack Joseon again in 1597. This time, however, the Ming-Joseon joint forces were better prepared to counter Japan (Pratt, and Rutt 1999:184). In 1598, Admiral Lee Soon-sin scored a decisive victory against Japan at the battle of Noryang. Admiral Lee of Joseon and Toyotomi Hideyoshi of Japan both died in the battle of Noryang that forced Japan to withdraw completely from Joseon (Pratt, and Rutt, 1999:184).

K-drama on Imjinwaeran

While several TV series and films depict the Japanese invasion of Joseon, Imjinwaeran (1592-1598 A.D.), most dramas focus on the life and achievements of the Admiral Lee Soon-sin who protected Joseon from the Japanese invaders. Some notable TV series and films on Admiral Lee include: "Immortal Admiral Lee Soon-sin" (불멸의 이순신) and "The Admiral: Roaring Currents".

	Title	Immortal Admiral Lee Soon-sin
	Production	Aired in 2004-2005 (104 episodes)
	Cast	Kim Myung-min, Lee Jae-ryong
	Synopsis	The drama follows General Lee's life story, starting from his childhood to his death. Focusing on Lee's military career, the drama also portrays political divisions within the court and the international relations surrounding Joseon at that time. (Poster © KBS)

Lee Soon-sin (1545-98) is famous for building the "geobooksun" (turtle ship), which had a protective covering, with numerous spikes embedded in the cover to prevent the enemy from boarding (Han 1995). Despite his military success, he fell victim to factional fights in the government and was removed from his post. With his charismatic leadership and employing the ironclad turtle ship, designed to withstand Japanese cannon fire, Admiral Lee's forces rammed and sank many Japanese ships. He died in the final battle of Noryang (Seth 2006:141).

Two most famous battles led by General Lee are the Noryang and Myeongryang battles. The movie, "Admiral: Roaring Currents," depicts the historical Battle of Myeongryang, that took place in October 1597. For the Myeonryang battle, Admiral Lee had only 13 warships, while Japan had a fleet of 133 ships. Against all odds, General Lee and the determined Korean soldiers defeated the Japanese fleet with the use of ingenious military tactics and naval maneuvers that later historians regard "one of the greatest military engagements of all time" in Korean history (KOCIS 2019).

	Title	The Admiral: Roaring Currents
	Production	Kim Han-min (director)/ Jeon Chul-hong (writer)/ Released in 2014
	Cast	Choi Min-sik, Ryu Seung-ryong, Cho Jin-woong
	Synopsis	Capitalizing on local knowledge about changing water flows of the Myeongryang Strait, Admiral Lee corners the Japanese fleet into a deadly trap. He then compounded the Japanese hardship by utilizing ingenious military maneuvers. (Poster © CJ Entertainment)

During the long period of wars (1592-1598), the Japanese invaders carried out extremely brutal atrocities against Koreans and Chinese soldiers. The Kyoto "Ear Mound" is a clear evidence of the Japanese gruesome acts during the imjinwaeran. The Japanese took ears and noses of 38,000 Koreans and Chinese soldiers and brought the body parts as war souvenirs to Japan. The dismembered body parts of the killed Koreans and Chinese were buried near a shrine commemorating Hideyoshi in Kyoto. Today, the burial site, known as "Mimizuka Ear Mound," is visited mainly by Korean and Chinese tourists (Seth 2006: 142).

About 126,000 Koreans were estimated to have been killed and some 60-70,000 people were taken to Japan as prisoners of war. During the 7 year-imjinwaeran period, the population of the capital, Seoul, fell from 100,000 to less than 40,000 (Pratt, and Rutt 1999:184). As the Japanese used a scorched earth tactic to terrorize the local population, the physical damage to property and cultural treasures was immense. Many cultural heritages in Joseon, including Bulguksa Temple in Gyeongju, were destroyed (KOCIS 2019). In contrast, the Korean captives, who were taken to Japan, greatly contributed to Japan's economic and cultural development, since many of the Korean captives were scholars, artisans, painters, ceramic craftsmen and expert type casters with special knowledge and skills (Seth 2006: 142; Pratt, and Rutt 1999:184).

Although it was China's suzerain obligation to defend Korea and also China's self-interest to secure its own border against the Japanese, the invaluable assistance of the Ming dynasty reinforced Korea's tributary ties and its emotional connection with the Ming court. The Joseon court built an altar to the Ming emperor Wanli, who had sent troops to support Korea against the Japanese (Seth 2006). The special Ming-Joseon relationship, however, became a source of political and diplomatic troubles that later fractured the Joseon court into various political factions.

Manchu Invasions (1627 -1636)

Only thirty years after the atrocious and devastating Japanese invasion, Joseon fell victim to yet another brutal invasion in 1627. This time, it was by the Manchu, a northern tribe in China. Conquering several tribes, the Manchus (also known as the Jurchen) emerged as a powerful force in 1616 and subsequently established the new state of Jin. The Manchu then began attacking the Ming dynasty that was ruled by the ethnic Han Chinese. As the Ming court called upon the king of Joseon for assistance, it was Joseon's turn to reciprocate the Ming's favour (Ming's earlier military support for Joseon during the imjinwaeran). As Joseon sided with the Ming, the Manchu (the

Jin dynasty) invaded Joseon in 1627. Soon, the Machu forces captured Pyeongyang and advanced south. Meantime, the Joseon king fled to Ganghwa Island. In 1636, the Manchus eventually defeated Korea and forced King Injo of Joseon to pledge his loyalty to the Manchus. Seven years later the Manchu also defeated the Ming dynasty of the Han Chinese and established the Qing dynasty in Beijing (Seth 2006: 142-143).

The Qing dynasty (the Manchu) forced the Koreans to pay for the war expenses as well as to pay a regular tribute. With Korean princes and members of the royal family taken as hostages by the Manchus, the Koreans were forced to accept their tributary status. Although Joseon remained a tributary state of the Qing dynasty for the next 350 years, Koreans harbored the feeling of animosity toward the Manchus. Albeit there was some gradual improvement in the Qing-Joseon relations over time, the Koreans felt more loyal to the former Ming dynasty and regarded the Qing rulers (the Manchus) as barbarian usurpers (Seth 2006).

Historical movies on the Manchu invasion		
The film, "Bow, The Ultimate Weapon" (also titled "War of the Arrows"), deals with the Manchu invasion. Set against the backdrop of the second Manchu invasion of 1636, the film depicts the plight of Koreans who had to defend themselves from the Manchu invaders.		
	Title	Bow, the Ultimate Weapon
	Production	2011 (Director: Kim Han-min)
	Cast	Park Hae-il, Ryoo Seung-yong
	Synopsis	The film tells a story of villagers who were attacked by the Manchu forces. A young bride in the village, captured by the Manchu invaders on her wedding day, is about to be taken as a slave to China. The film focuses on the fights between the Manchu invaders and the young bride's brother. Armed only with a bow and some arrows, he must use his archery skills to rescue his sister. (Poster © Lotte Entertainment)

Political Factionalism in the Joseon government after the Fall of the Ming Dynasty

Since the late 17th century, the Joseon court was characterized by rampant political factionalism (당쟁) that undermined the central government's ability to rule. Major political factions during the late Joseon period included dongin (동인 Easterners), bookin (북인 Northerners) and seoin (서인 Westerners).

The sources of factional struggles were diverse, but the ruling elite mainly fought over foreign policy and the succession to the throne. Some of their disputes traced back to the period prior to the Manchu invasion. While the bookin (Northerners) sought to avoid Joseon's involvement in the Manchu-Ming conflict, the seoin (Westerners) supported a pro-Ming policy. Foreign policy differences tend to intensify factionalism especially during the time of political crisis due to external threats. As for foreign policy issues, monarchs had to compete for political authority with powerful political factions in the court. The fierce competition among aristocratic factions often led to bloody purges (Seth 2006: 146). Political disagreements further divided the court into four factions, including the noron (노론 old doctrine) , seoron (서론 young doctrine), bookin (북인 northerners) and namin (남인 southerners).

The intensity of Korean factionalism was further fuelled by philosophical differences in neo-Confucianism and the divide was further entrenched by Confucian ethics that emphasizes loyalty to elders, superiors, and teachers (Seth 2006: 146). Against this political background, the silhak movement emerged in the 17th century, is the case in point. Highly critical of rigid neo-Confucian approaches, some Korean scholars advocated an alternative approach, called silhak (Practical Learning). According to rigid neo-Confucianism, wealth was thought to be derived from the land, while trade and commerce only diverted people from productive work (Seth 2006: 1913). In contrast, silhak scholars (such as Park Jiwon, Park Jega, Lee Tong Mu, and Jeon Yak-yong) criticized the lack of appreciation of the practical benefits of commerce and technology. In fact, despite the worldview of the conservative neo-Confucian aristocracy, the Joseon society had been slowly changing internally. Joseon's occupational mobility was on the rise, as more and more people became engaged in manufacturing and commercial activities[8].

Highly critical of the yangban's parasitic lifestyle and being aspired to build a more equitable and just society, silhak scholars advocated a land reform that would guarantee land to all peasants (Seth 2006: 146). The highly respected silhak scholar, Jeong Yak-yong (Tasan 1762-1836), called for an egalitarian redistribution of wealth (Seth 2006: 202) and the use of communally owned land. The silhak scholars argued that regardless of factional allegiance, people with appropriate knowledge and skills should be promoted to suitable positions (Pratt and Rutt 1999: p118). To change society, silhak scholars turned to education. They established many private institutions such as scowon and chongsa, challenging public colleges and other government schools (Joe, WJ 2000).

Historical fusion dramas on Joseon

Compared to classic historical dramas that focus on geo-politics, court intrigues and wars, historical fusion dramas have emerged as a subgenre of Sageuk (historical drama) that is more popular among younger viewers. The popularity of historical fusion drama is driven by many factors. First, it is less heavy on politics or actual historical events, as it predominantly revolves around melodramatic love stories or fantasies. Secondly, younger viewers find it more relatable to their life experience, as fusion dramas often utilize time travel and/or reincarnation elements that allow the crossing between the past and the present. Some fusion dramas draw on folktales and the folk literature from the Joseon time that are widely known among Korean people. The familiarity of popular folktales, revised to please contemporary viewers, makes fusion dramas easy to understand without much historical background knowledge.

---

[8] Although most foreign trade was limited by law to diplomatic missions, domestic commercial activities gradually increased, as evidenced by the fact that merchants and pedlars even formed a guild in the 17th century (Seth 2006: 195).

Historical Fusion Dramas on Joseon Kingdom

Some of the most popular fusion dramas that are set during the Joseon period include: The Legend of the Blue Sea, The Moon that embraces the Sun, Rooftop Prince, Faith, and Damo, among many others.

The TV series, "Rooftop Prince" is a historical fusion drama containing time-travel and reincarnation themes.

	Title	Rooftop Prince
	Production	Aired in 2012
	Cast	Park Yoochun and Han Ji Min
	Synopsis	A crown prince in Joseon time-travels to present day South Korea, while investigating the mysterious death of his wife. The crown prince and his bodyguards land in the rooftop apartment of Park Ha. While the prince feels attracted to her, he encounters a woman who looks identical to his late wife. (poster © SBS)

The TV series drama, "The Moon that embraces the Sun", tells a fictional story of black magic and fated love with the background of a political intrigue in the Joseon court.

	Title	The Moon that embraces the Sun
	production	Aired in 2012 (22 episodes)
	Cast	Kim Soo-hyeon and Han Ga-in
	Synopsis	The drama tells a fated love story between King Lee Hwon and a shaman, named Wol. The king enters into a loveless marriage relationship with a woman from an ambitious aristocratic family. A shaman is brought into the palace to cure the King's sickness. (poster © MBC)

The TV series, "Damo", is a historical fusion drama that revolves around a female police officer during the Joseon period. Focusing on her martial arts skills and intelligence, the drama tells a tragic story of love triangle.

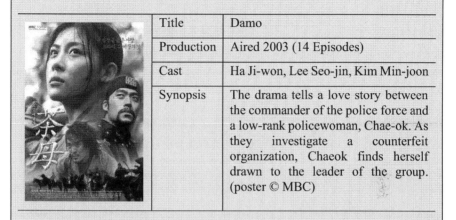

Title	Damo
Production	Aired 2003 (14 Episodes)
Cast	Ha Ji-won, Lee Seo-jin, Kim Min-joon
Synopsis	The drama tells a love story between the commander of the police force and a low-rank policewoman, Chae-ok. As they investigate a counterfeit organization, Chaeok finds herself drawn to the leader of the group. (poster © MBC)

The TV series, "My Love from the Star (별에서 온 그대)", tells a romantic love story about an alien and an reincarnated woman from Joseon.

Title	My Love from the Star
Production	Aired in 2014 (21 Episodes)
Cast	Jeon Ji-hyeon, Kim Soo-hyeon
Synopsis	The drama tells a fantasy story about an alien (Do Min-joon) who landed on Earth during the Joseon Dynasty period. He falls for a girl, but she dies while trying to help him. As an alien, Min-joon never ages. In present-day South Korea, he lives as a professor and meets Cheon Song-hi who looks identical to the girl that he loved 400 years ago. (poster © sbs)

> The drama was a major hit in South Korea and received immense popularity across Asia. It was broadcasted in many countries around the world.

Given that the Joseon kingdom lasted until the early 20th century, as the last monarchy on the Korean peninsula, numerous TV drams and films draw on historical events of Joseon as the main source of dramatization. For a long list of TV dramas and films on Joseon, please see the appendix at the end of the book.

Chapter 4

The Fall of Joseon

By the mid 19th century, Asia had become the site of international power rivalry. Britain forced China to accept a highly unequal trade treaty, after winning the infamous Opium War (1839-1842). The war was initiated by Britain after China cracked down on British drug trafficking in Beijing. Hong Kong became Britain's colony. Britain extracted more economic and political concessions from China after waging wars against China between 1858-1860 (Seth 2006).

Some major Atlantic powers (the USA, Britain, France, Germany) and Japan subjugated many countries under their colonial rule. Britain colonized India and Malaysia, while France occupied Vietnam, Laos, and Cambodia. The Netherlands conquered Indonesia. In 1898, the USA colonized the Philippines and the Hawaiian Islands (Oliver 1993: 91).

Table 4.1. Colonized countries in Asia in the 20th century

The Colonized	The Colonizer
China	Japan, Germany, France, Britain
Korea	Japan
Vietnam	France, Japan
Indonesia	Netherland
Malaysia & Singapore	Britain
India, Pakistan, Sri Lanka, Burma	Britain
The Philippines	Spain, USA
Laos & Cambodia	France

As in the case with China, some Atlantic powers deployed a "gunboat diplomacy" toward Korea and Japan, with the goal to obtain economic and political concessions by force. In 1854, the US succeeded in pressuring Japan to take an open-door policy. Japan, under a reform-oriented government, was quick to adapt to the changing international environment by importing modern technologies from Europe and the USA (Seth 2006). In contrast, Joseon was under an ultra-conservative government led by Daewongun[9]. Sticking to a close-door policy, Daewongun was adamant to keep all foreign countries (except China) away from Joseon. He enforced the isolationist policy by banning overseas travelling by Koreans and the entry of foreigners (Oliver 1993). For almost over two decades, Joseon under Daewongun resisted American and French attempts to set foot in Korea, as it withstood the French naval attack[10] in 1866 and the American naval campaign in 1871, despite suffering a large number of casualties.

The American Invasion of 1871

In May of 1871, American ships illegally entered Joseon's water to request a diplomatic and trade relationship with Joseon. When the Joseon court refused, the Americans attacked the forts on Ganghwa Island and killed about 350 Koreans. Facing Joseon's adamant "closed door" policy, the American ships eventually left Joseon without any diplomatic gains. The American invasion is also known as the Shinmiyangyo which means "the western disturbance in the *Shinmi* year".

Daewongun's policy of isolation continued throughout the 1860s and 70s, thus depriving Joseon of precious time and chances to modernize the country. In contrast to Joseon, Japan carried out political and economic reform measures to modernize the country. With the adoption of modern technology

---

[9] Daewongun was the father of King Gojong (r. 1864-1907). When Gojong ascended to the throne in 1864, he was only 12 years old. This allowed his father to act as, de facto, the ruler of Joseon.

[10] In the mid-19th century, some Korean Catholics and foreign missionaries were persecuted in Joseon. In retaliation, France attacked Korean forts on Ganghwa island with its naval force.

and by centralizing its political system, Japan soon emerged as a powerful military state by the end of 19th century.

The Japanese invasion of 1875 and the unequal Gwanghwa Treaty

Taking advantage of the declining power of China (Korea's traditional ally), Japan invaded Joseon in 1875 with only three ships! Killing 35 Koreans on Gwanghwa and Yeongjong islands, Japan threatened the Joseon court with a full-scale warfare, if Seoul refused to open its door to Japan. King Gojong (r. 1864-1907) agreed to the Japanese demand by signing an unequal trade agreement with Japan. The Gwanghwa treaty in 1876 was extremely disadvantageous to Joseon, for it granted numerous extraterritorial privileges to the Japanese. For instance, the Japanese did not have to pay any taxes for their import and exports, while using their own currency for trading in Joseon (Seth 2006; Oliver 1993).

The Gwanghwa treaty of 1876 granted Japanese citizens:

- the right of free passage throughout Korea
- the right to trade without paying import or export taxes
- the right to use three ports (Busan, Incheon, and Wonsan)
- the right of Japanese citizens in Korea to be tried by the Japanese judiciary
- the right to use their own currency in Korean ports
- the posting of Japanese consuls in trading ports
- the right to establish diplomatic missions in Seoul (Pratt and Rutt 1999: Oliver 1993)

From 1875 onward, Japan carried out a series of military and diplomatic campaigns to turn Joseon into Japan's colony. The first step toward Japan's imperial ambition was to secure Japan's access to Joseon's markets as well as the influx of Japanese settlers to Korea. The Gwanghwa treaty of 1876 guaranteed this precondition for Japan's colonization of Joseon. The next step was to diplomatically and militarily undermine Joseon's allies (notably China and Russia), while rallying support from some Korean elites and major Atlantic powers, especially the USA and Britain.

Political Division in Joseon's government: Divided Elite

Joseon's isolationist foreign policy came to an end with the Japanese invasion of 1875 and the resulting Gwanghwa Treaty of 1876. Although Joseon's ruling elites had been trying to change the country's foreign policy, the government was too divided to push forward coherent policies. The ruling elite of Joseon was largely divided into two camps, the pro-China and the pro-Japan groups, as they clashed over the degree of economic and societal liberalization. While both King Gojong and Queen Min (Empress Myeonseong) favored economic and political reform measures, Daewongun and neo-Confucian scholars opposed the modernization policy.

Daewongun versus Queen Min

The TV series dramas, "Daewongun" and "Splendid Dawn" (찬란한 여명), shed light on the life of Daewongun, the father of King Gojong. Several dramas and movies depicting Queen Min also exist. They include: The China-Japan War and Queen Min (청일전쟁과 여걸민비), Poong-un (풍운), Empress Myeong-sung (명성황후) and The Sword with No Name.

	Title	Empress Myeong Sung (명성황후)
	Production	Aired in 2001 (KBS)
	cast	Choi Myeong-gil
	Synopsis	The drama depicts the politics of the late Joseon court with the focus on Queen Min and Daewongun. (Poster KBS)

The film, "The Sword with No Name" (불꽃처럼 나비처럼), depicts the life of Queen Min and her political struggle against her rival factions in the court.

	Title	The Sword with No Name
	Production	2009 (directed by Kim Yong-gyun)
	cast	Jo Seung-woo, Soo Ae
	Synopsis	The film tells a fictional love story involving Queen Min and her bodyguard. (Poster ©Showbox)

The reformers were further divided into divergent camps, depending on which foreign countries they looked up to as a reliable ally and a reform-model to emulate. Seeking to modernize Joseon, Queen Min and her political supporters relied on China and politically crashed with the conservative pro-Daewongun forces. Other reformers in the government (such as Park Yong-hyo and Kim Ok-kywun) looked to Japan as a reform model and opposed Queen Min's pro-China faction. Some Koreans looked favorably to Russia or the USA in order to counter Japan's increasing influence in Joseon.

Hoping that other foreign powers could counter Japan's growing dominance in Joseon, King Gojong established diplomatic and trade relations with the USA, Russia, and France. With the signing of a trade agreement with Joseon, American businesses obtained various economic gains including mining concessions and the contract for building an electricity-driven street lighting system as well as Asia's first street railway system in Seoul (Oliver 1993: 61).

King Gojong began experimenting with a series of modernization measures including the creation of the first Korean newspaper and the reform of the Korean army (Pratt and Rutt 1999: 187). After the diplomatic treaty with the USA in 1882, Joseon allowed foreign missionaries to set up schools and churches (Seth 2006:223). Gojong appointed Horace Allen (an American missionary) as an advisor to the royal court and set up an English school in the king's palace. In 1895, the government expanded the Foreign Language school (Japanese, French, Russian, Chinese, German, English) to enhance Korean diplomatic capabilities by providing government officials with more informed knowledge on international relations.

The Influx of Foreign Culture and Technology

Many TV dramas and films on Korea at the turn of the 20th century depict the influx of European culture and technology. The TV series drama, "Mr. Sunshine", contains many episodes that depict the changing urban landscape of the late Joseon. The changes included the establishment of railways and the use of electricity. The drama also depicts the role of European and American missionaries in the proliferation of Christian schools in the late Joseon society. As of 1909, it was recorded that the number of Christian schools at the middle and high school level numbered around 950 (Joe, WJ 2000: 719).

The TV series, "Jejungwon: the Hospital (제중원)", depicts the first European style hospital, that was established in 1885 during the reign of King Gojong. Jejungwon later developed into the present-day Yonsei Severance Hospital. The drama tells the stories about the first Korean doctor trainees at the hospital. The main character in the drama is loosely based on a real historical figure, Park Seo-yang who graduated from Jejungwon and became a doctor despite his "cheonmin" class background. After Japan colonized Joseon, Park joined the Korea Independence Movement.

	Title	Jejungwoon: the Hospital
	Production	Aired in 2010 (36 episodes)
	cast	Han Hye-jin, Park Yong-woo
	Synopsis	The drama tells a story of a young man who becomes a doctor despite his low social status. He faces numerous challenges from his rivals. (Poster ©SBS)

Some conservative Korean elites were discontented with King Gojong's new foreign policy and his liberalization measures. Together with conservative military officers, they waged a coup and tried to bring back the conservative former ruler, Daewongun, to power. To crush the coup attempt, King Gojong and Queen Min asked for a Chinese intervention. The Chinese government sent 4000 troops into Korea and captured Daewongun. He was later sent to China into his exile (Oliver 1993: 59).

Meanwhile, the political conflict within the government did not end with the failed coup led by the conservative traditional elite. This time, the pro-Japan reformers, led by Kim Ok-kyun, sought to get rid of the pro-China faction in the royal court. With the support of the Japanese, the pro-Japan faction organized a coup d'état (known as the Kapsin coup) in December 1884. As in the case with the coup by the traditional camp, the pro-Japan reformers' coup also failed, as China intervened again to the aid of Queen Min (Maddonald, 1996:37).

The pro-China faction of the reformers suggested Paul Georg von Moellendorf (a German), as an advisor to the royal court. Moellendorf tried to initiate a radical reform program which included building railways and the import and employment of modern machinery. He recommended the use of Hangeul in schools and general publication, as well as tax reform to reduce the power of the yangban class (Oliver 1993: 59). Although Moellendorf was initially recommended by China, he favorably viewed Russia as a more promising ally than China, in terms of helping Joseon to counterbalance Japan's power. Thus, he tried to persuade King Gojong to side with Russia (Oliver 1993: 59). As Moellendorf's pro-Russia policy upset the pro-China reformers, they had Moellendorf be replaced with Yuan Shih-kai, a Chinese Resident General, in 1885 (Lee KB, 1984: 61).

Donghak Revolution

After two failed coups by different political factions, challenges to the royal court came from below. Political discontent in Joseon was widespread. The masses of the commoners were unhappy about their economic hardship, exacerbated by corrupt government officials, and power rivalry in the government as well as the presence of foreign powers, especially the growing Japanese influence in Joseon. Against this political backdrop, the Donghak (동학 Eastern Learning) philosophy, first developed by Choe Je-woo in 1860, provided an ideological foundation for the powerful political movement of the Korean masses. Donghak ideology, selectively drawing on ideas from Confucianism, Buddhism, and Daoism, advocates an egalitarian society based on meritocracy and social justice. Although Donghak is not a religion in the sense that it does not promise an afterlife, it developed into a quasi-religion with the founder's written work as the bible of the Donghak movement.

As Donghak called for sweeping social reform, the Joseon court tried to suppress it by executing the founder and some important followers in 1864. The persecution, however, resulted in more converts and the expansion of the Donghak movement (Seth 2006; Oliver 1993). The Korean farmers, inspired by the Donghak ideology, demanded that the royal court eradicate corruption in the government and carry out a sweeping social and political reform. Their demands were as follows:

- suppression of official corruption,
- the abolition of slavery,
- the abolition of traditional hierarchical distinctions,

- the right of widows to remarry,
- equitable distribution of farmlands,
- the punishment of all who had collaborated with the Japanese (Oliver, 1993:66).

As their demands fell on deaf ear, the Korean farmers erupted in an armed uprising in 1894. After a series of battles that dealt a serious blow to the government troops, King Gojong finally agreed to make some concessions to the Donghak farmers. After the King assured that their demands would be met, the Donghak followers put down arms and dispersed.

K-Drama on the Donghak Revolution

The TV series, "Mung Bean Flower (녹두꽃)", depicts the socio-political circumstances of the Donghak peasant revolution which took place in 1894. While the drama sheds light on the suffering of the poor Korean farmers at the hands of corrupt government officials, it also portrays the collusion between the corrupt Korean elite and the Japanese imperialists.

	Title	Mung Bean Flower
	Production	Aired in 2019 (48 episodes)
	cast	Jo Jung-suk, Yoon Si-yoon, Han Ye-ri
	Synopsis	The drama revolves around the lives of two half-brothers who find themselves deeply involved in the 1894 Donghak Peasant Movement. (Poster ©SBS)

In this context, Gojong introduced progressive social reform measures (Gabbo reforms) which formally abolished slavery and the traditional class distinctions. The Gabbo Reforms of 1894 included the following measures:

- abolition of slavery,

- a revised examination system based on modern subjects such as mathematics, international relations and expansion of the school system,
- the establishment of an independent judiciary system,
- giving the yangban the right to engage in trade,
- ending of child marriage and the neo-Confucian prohibition on widow remarriage (Pratt and Rutt 1999: 194-195)

Geo-political Rivalry in Asia

At the outbreak of the Donghak rebellion, Queen Min and her pro-China faction asked Beijing for help. As the Donghak leaders struck a deal with King Gojong, the Donghak rebellion came to an end before the Chinese troops arrived. Exploiting the political instability of Joseon resulting from the Donghak Peasant Rebellion, Japan seized the opportunity to strengthen its control of Joseon.

The First Sino-Japanese War of 1894

Japan regarded China its main rival over Joseon and used the political instability surrounding the Donghak rebellion as an occasion to get rid of Chinese influence on the Joseon government. Under the pretext of helping Joseon and ensuring the safety of Japanese residents, Japan dispatched 8000 soldiers to Joseon. As mentioned early, since the Donghak leaders reached an agreement with King Gojong, the Joseon court asked all foreign troops to leave the country. Japan, however, refused to withdraw its troops in defiance of Gojong's order, and instead used its troops to mount military attacks on China. The first Sino-Japan war of 1894 was initiated by Japan to gain hegemony over Joseon against China (Oliver, 1993:66).

The First Sino-Japanese war lasted for a year and resulted in Japan's victory in 1895. China was forced to sign the Treaty of Shimonoseki that would end the Sino-Joseon alliance. After the Sino-Japanese War, Japan deported all Chinese residents from Korea (Oliver, 1993:67) and demanded the Joseon court to end even its bilateral trade relations with China. When Gojong refused Japan's demand, Japanese troops occupied the royal palace and arrested King Gojong in July 1895. Japan disarmed the Korean Army and had Korea's weaponry turned over to the Japanese army (Oliver, 1993:66). Replacing King Gojong, Japan set up a pro-Japanese puppet government, ironically headed by Gojong's father, the conservative Daewongun, who turned to a pro-Japan collaborator and promised to ensure Japan's control over Korea's domestic affairs. The pro-Japan puppet government granted Japan many exclusive commercial contracts including the right to build railways and a telegraph system and the right to use all Jeolla coastal ports for Japanese ships (Oliver 1993).

Furthermore, Japan sent its secret agents to assassinate Queen Min, the most influential leader of the pro-China reform faction in the Joseon court. In October 1895, the Japanese agents killed Queen Min and three of her attendants. The assassins burnt the bodies of Queen Min and of her companions to destroy the evidence of their crime. To cover up their crime, the Japanese authority publicly announced that Queen Min had committed treason and vanished without a trace. Despite Japan's efforts to silence press reports on the murder of Queen Min, the truth finally leaked. The wives of foreign missionaries, who were the Queen's friends, wrote to their homes about the murder, and the Japanese assassination of Queen Min finally came to light.

After Japan's brutal killing of Queen Min, King Gojong fled to the Russian legation in Seoul. Fearing for his life, the king lived there in the protection of the Russian Embassy for one year (from February 1896 until February 1897). Meanwhile, outraged by the Japanese murder of Queen Min, many Koreans initiated armed uprisings against the Japanese forces in Joseon. Calling themselves as Eubyeung (the Righteous Army), taking the name of the popular people's militia that fought against the Japanese during the Imjinwaeran in 1592-1599, the Koreans against the pro-Japan government and the supporters of the Donghak movement fought against the Japanese forces in Joseon between December 1895 and January 1896 (Oliver, 1993;67).

While Joseon was in the midst of political turmoil, some European countries came together to put a brake on Japan's imperial ambition. Alarmed by Japan's growing control of East Asia, three European powers (Russia, France, and Germany) issued a tripartite warning against the Japanese forces in China and Korea (Oliver, 1993:68). Russia, in particular, strongly opposed

Japan's control of Joseon. The tripartite intervention finally enabled King Gojong to restore his reign and dismissed the pro-Japanese puppet administration. After King Gojong returned to the palace in 1897, he changed the name of the country from Joseon to the Great Han Empire (대한제국). The name change was largely symbolic. By proclaiming the Joseon kingdom as an empire, Gojong hoped to assert Korea's diplomatic independence from Japan and his counterpart, the Japanese emperor (Oliver 1993).

Looking for dependable allies to counter Japan, King Gojong favorably looked to Russia for support. In May 1896, he sent Queen Min's brother to Moscow to forge a close economic and political tie with Russia. Thanks to Russia's growing influence on Gojong and his government officials, Russia obtained some economic concessions including the right to use the ports of Busan and Masan and the right to exploit the timber resources in northern Korea in 1901 (Oliver 1993: 91). Gojong continued the open-door policy but hoped that other foreign powers, especially Russia, would keep Japan's aggression in check.

The Anglo-Japan Treaty of 1902: British Support for Japan's Control of Joseon

To Gojong's dismay, Japan succeeded in making political alliances with major Atlantic powers to diplomatically isolate Korea. First, Japan made an alliance with Britain in 1902. The Anglo-Japan Alliance of 1902, which was renewed twice in 1905 and 1921, secured British support for Japan's colonization of Korea.

Anglo-Japanese Alliance (Photo: Public Domain)

The Anglo-Japanese Treaty stated that Britain recognized Japan's paramount rights in Korea, and that would not seek a restoration of Korea's independence. In return, the treaty confirms that Japan would acknowledge Britain's control of India (Pratt and Rutt 1999: 13).

In addition to the Anglo-Japan alliance, Japan also secured tacit support from Washington, although a formal written agreement came only later in the form of the Taft-Katsura Agreement in 1905.

The Russo-Japanese War of 1904

Having secured British and American complicity or their acquiescence, Japan was emboldened to challenge Russia over Korea. In 1903, Japan demanded that Russia accept the Japanese control of Korea. When Russia refused, Japan launch military attacks on Russia in 1904, by utilizing its troops in Korea. The Russo-Japanese War lasted for over a year and ended with Japan's victory in 1905. About 90,000 Russians and 71,000 Japanese died in the war. In 1905, Russia was forced to sign the Treaty of Portsmouth that entailed Russian acknowledgement of Japan's control of Korea (Oliver 1993: 92-93).

The Taft-Katsura Memorandum of 1905: American support for Japan's control of Joseon

As the Russo-Japanese war was near to the end, Japan signed a memorandum with the United States of America over the question of Korea's sovereignty. Known as the Taft-Katsura Memorandum of 1905, it was signed by William Howard Taft, Secretary of War of the USA, and Japan's Prime Minster Katsura Taro. According to the memorandum which was re-confirmed by President Roosevelt, the USA viewed that "the establishment by Japanese troops of a suzerainty over Korea to the extent of requiring that Korea enter into no foreign treaties without the consent of Japan was the logical result of the present war and would directly contribute to permanent peace in the East" (Oliver 1993: 93). In return for American support, Japan assured that it would not oppose the American control of the Philippines (Pratt and Rutt 1999: 459). In other words, Japan and the USA made a geopolitical deal that they would not interfere in each other's respective sphere of influence.

American rivalry with Russia played a major role in the forging of the US-Japan alliance. As in the case with the British, the American administration under Theodore Roosevelt held the view that Japan could function as a counterforce to Russia and that Japan's control over Korea in this context would be beneficial to the USA (Oliver 1993).

Geopolitical interests largely shaped the pro-Japanese attitudes of the British and American governments. The ignorance of Europeans and Americans about Joseon and her relations with Japan also played an important role in their polices toward Joseon. Americans and Europeans obtained (mis)information about Korea, as they mainly relied on pro-Japanese publications such as *Corea, The Hermit Nation,* written by William Elliot Griffis. The author, who never visited Korea but only lived in Japan between 1870 and 1874, published numerous books and articles disparaging toward Koreans. The writer, while extolling Japan, argued that "Korea was too small and weak to be considered a separate entity and that its people would be best served by its becoming a protectorate of Japan" (Oliver 1993: 57). Between 1882 and 1911, for three decades, Griffin's book was widely circulated and greatly influenced the formation of Euro-American attitudes toward Korea (Oliver 1993: 57).

What Griffin and others did not understand was the extent of Korean resentment and their deep-seated hostility toward Japan, stemming from the repeated Japanese aggressions (Imjinwaeran in the 16th century and its naval attack in 1875). They also underestimated Koreans' national pride. Having a 5000-year-old history of independent Korean kingdoms, Koreans regarded themselves as being culturally superior to the "barbarian" Japanese who used to import cultural and technological know-how from various Korean kingdoms over centuries. Contrary to what the US-Japan memorandum stated, if Korea becomes Japan's protectorate, it would not "directly contribute to permanent peace in the East" but rather it would unleash violent conflicts since the Japanese rule over Korea would be resolutely opposed by the proud Koreans.

After defeating China and Russia in 1895 and 1904 respectively and with the political support from Britain and the USA, Japan emerged as the dominant power on the Korean peninsula. Other European powers such as France and Germany became largely acquiescent to the Japanese annexation of Korea, since Japan had a backing of British and American powers. It is one thing to challenge Japan, but challenging Japan's powerful allies would be a totally different game. At the end of the day, the changing geo-political alliances in Asia forced other Atlantic Powers to make a different political calculus about helping Korea. The tripartite power configuration (Britain-USA- Japan) was crucial for the rise and fall of Japan in East Asia. When Japan's former allies (Britain and the USA) turned against Japan by joining forces with Russia and China by the end of WWII, Japan's occupation of Korea could no longer sustain.

Table 4.2 Japan's foreign relations and Japan's military and diplomatic campaigns to colonize Korea

Country	Relations with Japan	Major political events	Outcome
China	Rivalry /Hostile	Sino-Japan War and the Treaty of Shimonoseki in 1895	Removing Chinese influence from Korea
Russia	Rivalry/ Hostile	Russo-Japanese War of 1904-5	Removing Russian influence from Korea
Britain	Japan's Ally	Anglo-Japanese Treaty (1902 and 1905)	British support for Japan's colonization of Korea
The USA	Japan's ally	Taft memorandum of 1905	American support for Japan's colonization of Korea
Others (France, Germany)	Rivalry / Later complicit		Complicit in Japan's colonization of Korea

The Protectorate Treaty of 1905 and the Loss of Joseon's Sovereignty

The Anglo-Japanese Alliance, the US-Japan Agreement (the Taft-Katsura Memorandum), and Japan's military victory over China and Russia, all paved the way for Japan's annexation of Korea. The only remaining obstacle was the resistance of the Korean people. In November 1905, Ito Hirobumi (a Japanese government official) entered the royal palace in Korea with Japanese troops. He demanded that King Gojong accept a treaty which would make Joseon a protectorate of Japan. When King Gojong refused to sign, he was taken by Japanese soldiers to be locked away temporarily. Several ministers of the government wavered and gave in. They signed the treaty at the gunpoint.

The Protectorate Treaty deprived Korea of its diplomatic sovereignty. Korea could no longer make diplomatic exchanges with foreign governments without Japan's permission. Under this treaty, a Japanese resident-general would also take charge of Korean domestic affairs (Oliver 1993: 95).

Refusing to accept the treaty, King Gojong sought to expose the illegality of the protectorate treaty to the international community. He turned to foreign governments for help, as he tried to nullify the treaty that Japan imposed on Korea by force. In October 1905, King Gojong sent a letter to President Roosevelt, asking for American help but in vain. Again, in November 1905, Gojong sent his message (via his former advisor, Hulbert) to the American government, explaining that the protectorate treaty was forced upon Korea "at the point of the sword and under duress" and that Gojong "never consented to it and never will." Completely ignoring the desperate plea from Gojong, the American government refused to accept the King's letter (Oliver 1993:96). Nonetheless, Min Yong-hwan (a government minister and a nephew of the slain Queen Min) and Prime Minster Han Kyu made yet another desperate appeal to the President of the USA. When the Korean delegates asked for a meeting with the Secretary of State, the American authority told them that they would need Japan's permission. After their failed attempt to garner support from Washington, Min Yong-hwan committed suicide in protest. A dozen or more Korean officials and scholars followed suit by committing suicide in protest against the 1905 protectorate treaty (Oliver 1993).

Koreans did not give up their hope of obtaining international support for Korea's claim of independence. In June 1907, Gojong secretly sent an envoy to the Second International Peace Conference at the Hague to present Korean claim to independence[11]. Siding with Japan, however, the major Atlantic powers barred the Korean delegates from even entering the conference on the ground that without Japanese permission, the Korean delegates had no authority to speak on behalf of Korea. Yi Chun, one of the Korean delegates, committed suicide in protest (Oliver 1993:96-97).

In retaliation to Gojong's attempt to claim Korea's independence at the Hague Peace Conference, Japan forced Gojong to abdicate and put his son, Sunjong, on the throne. One month later, in August 1907, Japan issued a decree to disband the Korean Army (Pratt and Rutt 1999). Defying the dissolution order, Korean soldiers fought against the Japanese forces. The main fighting took place at the Gate of Namdaemun in Seoul and the battle resulted in many Korean casualties.

The Battle of Namdaemun in 1907. (Public Domain)

---

[11] Together with Homer Hulbert, the Korean delegates to the Hague conference included Yi Chun (prosecutor of the Supreme Court) and Yi Sang-sol (a former cabinet officer).

Many of the survivors of the Namdaemun battle and the members of the disbanded Korean Army fled to China or Russia, to join the Korean people's militia, called "eubyeong" (the Righteous Army).

K-drama and films on the Battle of Namdaemun Gate

The Battle of Namdaemun Gate is depicted in the TV series drama, "Mr. Sunshine". Portraying the political circumstances surrounding the dissolution of the Korean Army, shortly after Emperor Gojong's forced abdication in July 1907, the drama depicts the brutality of the Japanese forces through the eyes of a fictional figure, an American military officer, Eugene Choi.

In the drama, "Mr. Sunshine", Eugene Choi, the main male character in the drama, secretly helps Eubyeong (the Righteous Army). He is temporarily entrusted by King Gojong to train Koreans at the Academy of the Korean Imperial Army. When the Korean Army was forced to be disbanded, he witnessed many of his former students killed by the Japanese Army.

With the Japanese colonization of Korea still being the most painful national trauma, many Koreans frequently return to the historical time period of the end of the Joseon dynasty, in order to find answers to why Joseon fell victim to Japanese imperial ambition. Reflecting the public interest, a large body of films and TV dramas on the fall of Joseon is available.

Table 4.3 K-dramas and films on the fall of Joseon

Taeyangin Lee Je-ma (태양인 이제마), The Merchant: Gaekju (장사의 신), Gunman in Joseon (조선총잡이), Je Jung Won (제중원), Byeolsungeom (조선과학 수사대 별순검), Mr. Sunshine (미스터 선샤인), The Sword with No Name (불꽃처럼 나비처럼), The Righteous Army: The Age of Heroes (의군: 푸른 영웅의 시대), Myeongsung-hwanghoo (명성황후), Daewongun (대원군), Splendid Dawn (찬란한 여명), The Land (토지), Gabi (가비), Mung Bean Flower (녹두꽃)

Chapter 5

Colonized Korea and the National Movement for Korea's Independence

---

This chapter provides an overview of the Japanese atrocities against Koreans during the Japanese occupation of Korea (1910-1945), followed by a history of the movement for Korea's independence. It also provides snippets of information on some selected TV dramas and films relevant to the historical events under review.

The Japanese Rule of Korea

Five years after the protectorate treaty of 1905, Japan fully incorporated Korea into its expanding colonial empire. In 1910, Japan tried to force King Sunjong to sign the treaty of Japan's annexation, that would grant Japan full control of Korea. Facing King Sunjong's refusal, Resident-General of Japan had Sunjong removed by force and signed the treaty together with the pro-Japan collaborator, Prime Minister Lee Wan-Yong. King Sunjong was forced to abdicate and lived under Japanese surveillance until he died in 1926.

The Japanese rule was brutal and humiliating to Koreans. The Japanese colonial government plundered Korea's land and resources, while destroying Korean culture and dignity. The following is a brief summary of some of the most atrocious crimes perpetrated by the Japanese occupying forces against the Korean people.

Dispossession, Resources Extraction & Industrialization for Japan's Imperialist Expansion

Japan outright expropriated the land of many Koreans and their properties without compensation. Even well before Japan's formal annexation of Korea, the Japanese authority dispossessed the homes of about 15,000 families in and around Seoul for a "military necessity" (Oliver 1993:94). Once Korea became part of the Japanese empire, hundreds and thousands of Japanese landless farmers came to Korea and seized the land and properties of many Korean farmers and the yangban. As for land ownership, about 3 per cent of Korea's arable land in 1910 already belonged to the Japanese settlers in Korea. Twenty years later, Japanese landownership increased to 60 percent as of 1930. By 1940, the Japanese settlers in Korea numbered more than 708,000 (Oliver 1993: 120).

Japanese companies such as the Oriental Development Company and the Fuji Industrial Company were given the power to expropriate all land and properties in Korea (Oliver 1993: 120). Japanese corporations exploited all Korean mineral and timber resources. More than 90 percent of Korea's mines and a majority of all factories in Korea eventually belonged to Japanese enterprises, while the Korean-operated industries were either outright prohibited or remained very primitive (Pratt, and Rutt 1999; Joe WJ, 2002: 779). With the expropriated land and properties, the Japanese pillaged Joseon's resources and exploited the impoverished Koreans as cheap labor (or forced labor) for Japanese companies. The supply of Korean coal and iron, together with the import of other important minerals absent in Japan, paved the way for Japan's rapid economic development and its military campaigns. At the same time, the construction of public infrastructures such as railways and ports in Korea was done to serve Japan's military ambition toward the colonization of Asia. In essence, the industrialization of Korea under the Japanese largely benefited the Japanese colonial expansion and its war efforts in Asia (Oliver 1993: 149).

Forced Migration and Slavery: "Stolen Country, Abducted People"[12]

Japan's colonization of Korea led to the uprooting and the enslaving of Koreans. Several million Koreans were forced to leave their own country, as they fled to escape political persecution, poverty, slavery and military conscription. Many of the Korean refugees fled to China and Russia. Between 1910 and 1944, about 300,000 Koreans emigrated to Siberia (Oliver 1993: 149). By 1910, some 200,000 Koreans lived in Manchuria. In 1925, the number of Korean refugees in Manchuria increased to 530,000. By 1940, the Korean refugees numbered over 1.4 million people (Oliver 1993: 122).

As for the total number of Korean residents in Japan, it numbered around 2 million by 1945 (Oliver 1993:122). While some Korean elite voluntarily emigrated to Japan to seek better educational opportunities, most Koreans in Japan were either poor refugees or industrial conscripts (forced labor) who were brought to work at dangerous workplaces in Japan. Beginning in the 1930s and until the end of WWII, conscripted Korean civilians and Chinese prisoners of war (POWs) were forced to work in Japan's industrial, mining, and shipbuilding sites. Between 1938 and 1945, 45% of all Koreans, who were taken to Japan against their will, had to work at coal mines. For instance, 9,300 Koreans were forced to work at the Miike (마이케) coal mines, while over one thousand Korean people were enslaved to work at Hashima and Dakashima coal mines in Japan (Kim MC et.al. 2018). Koreans were mobilized against their will to construct roads, ships, airports, and various industrial and military infrastructure in Japan and Japan's colonies such as Taiwan. About 7000 Koreans were forced to build underground tunnels in Japan (Kim SU, 2019: 214). Between 1943 and 1944, about 200 Koreans were taken to Taiwan, Japan's colony at that time, to be forced to extract resources and to build roads (Kim MC, et.al. 2018). Korean women were also taken to Japan to be forced to work at various factories producing military equipment. Between 1944 and 1945, more than one thousand Korean girls were forced to work for Tomaya Fujikoshi (도야마 후지코시) company, while about 600 worked for Asaito Numaz company in Tokyo (누마즈 도쿄 아사이토) and Mitsubishi Airport manufacturing company in Nagoya in 1944 (Kim MC. et.al., 2018). It is estimated that about 660,000

---

[12] Kim Min-cheol, et.al. (2018) *Battleship Island. The Unfinished War*. Saenggak-jeongwon.

Korean men and women were forced to work for Japanese corporations and the Japanese government (Kim MC, et.al., 2018).

Among hundreds and thousands of Koreans who were forced to work for various Japanese corporations, some 6000 Koreans had to work for the Mitsubishi Ship building company in Nagasaki alone (Kim HG 2017). In 1945, about 70,000 people out of the total 690,000 victims of the US atomic bomb in Nagasaki, were Koreans (Kim MC, et.al. 2018). This high number of Korean victims is indicative of the situation in which a huge number of conscripted Koreans worked in Japan's industrial center, Nagasaki, when the USA dropped atomic bombs at the end of the World War II.

Since Japan has refused to acknowledge the full extent of its atrocious acts against the Koreans during its occupation of Korea, most Koreans, quite understandably, have expressed their anger at the lack of Japan's remorse.

The Battleship Island and the Korean Slaves in Japan

The film "The Battleship Island" sheds a critical light on the still unresolved issue between Korea and Japan over wartime forced labor.

	Title	The Battleship Island
	Production Director/ Writer	Released in 2017 Ryoo Seung-wan/Ryoo Seung-wan, Shin Kyung-il
	Cast	Hwang Jung-min, So Ji-sub, Song Joong-ki, Lee Jung-hyun
	Synopsis	The film depicts the brutal treatment of Koreans and the deplorable conditions under which Koreans were forced to work on Japan's Hashima island. The film dramatizes mostly real historical events by spicing up with some fictional stories involving a secret rescue mission of an infiltrated Korean agent and a mass escape attempt. (Poster © CJ Entertainment)

The film, "The Battleship Island", is based on the true story about the Koreans who were forced to work for Mitsubishi company at the coal mines on Japan's Hashima island, off the coast of Nagasaki. With the

---

island resembling a ship, it was also known as the Battleship Island. The island, which Mitsubishi owned until 2002, is currently under the jurisdiction of Nagasaki City. During World War II, hundreds and thousands of Koreans were forced to work in coal mines on the island. It is estimated that about 1,300 of those slave workers died on the island due to the brutal treatment by the Japanese.

In 2015, Mitsubishi corporation made a formal apology to American prisoners of war (POWs) who were forced to work for the company during World War II (The Diplomat, 21 July 2015). About 12,000 American POWs were forced to work at mining sites or industrial plants in Japan. As one of the American prisoners in such a camp recalls, "It was slavery in every way: no food, no medicine, no clothing, no sanitation." Due to the ill-treatment of POWs, it was estimated that about 10 percent of American POWs died in Japanese labor camps (The Diplomat, 21 July 2015). Although the American prisoners of war (POWs) received an apology for their slave labor and the brutal treatment, neither the Japanese government nor the company has apologized to Korean and Chinese victims.

In 2005, the families of both Chinese and Korean victims filed lawsuits seeking a formal apology and compensation for the atrocious treatment at Japanese factories and mines during the war (The Diplomat, 21 July 2015). In October 2018, South Korea's Supreme Court ruled in favor of the Korean victims by ordering Mitsubishi to pay compensation. Angrily responding to the Korean verdict, the Japanese government warned of negative consequences (Reuters, 30 October 2018). When the South Korean government refused to interfere into the court ruling, Japan's Abe administration sought to punish South Korea by inflicting economic pains. Japan has initiated a trade war against South Korea by banning the export of Japanese products that are crucial ingredients for the production of semiconductors, Korea's top export item.

During the Asia-Pacific War, many Koreans were conscripted into the Japanese military to become its cannon fodder (Oliver, 1993:153). Between 1939 and 1945, some 800,000 Korean youths were drafted into Japan's imperial armed forces (Oliver 1993: 122).

During the Asia-Pacific War, hundreds and thousands of Korean women were forced into sexual slavery for Japanese soldiers (Pratt and Rutt 1999: 82). The Japanese authority put many Korean women in "comfort stations", the euphemism for Japanese brothels, in its colonies. Between 1943 and 1945 alone, it was estimated that about 200,000 Korean women were forced into sexual slavery (Kim SU, 2019: 228). While the total number of "comfort women" from Japan's colonies was estimated to be around 500,000 (Blakenmore 2018), more than 80 per cent of the enslaved women were taken from Korea (Kim SU, 2019: 227).

Korean "comfort women" (Source: Asian Women's Fund)

The "Comfort Women" Issue

Several films deal with the "comfort women", a thorny historical issue between Korea and Japan. Although Koreans demand a sincere apology from Japan, the Japanese government (under the conservative Liberal Democratic Party) has refused to acknowledge Japan's responsibility for its crimes against humanity including the sexual slavery. Japan even furiously reacts to the Korean campaign to erect statues to commemorate the "comfort women" in public places.

	Title	Spirits' Homecoming (귀향)
	Director	Cho Jeong-rae (Released in 2016)
	Cast	Gang Han-na, Choi Ri
	Synopsis	"Spirit's Homecoming" is about the Korean "comfort women." The film focuses on two Korean teenagers who were kidnapped by the Japanese to be sent to a "comfort station". (Poster © Jo Entertainment)

While the "Sprits Homecoming" is a commercial film, several documentary films including "My Name is Kim Bok-dong" are also available.

	Title	My Name is Kim Bok-dong.
	Production	Released in 2019
	Synopsis	This documentary film tells the real story of Kim Bok-dong, a "comfort woman". She organized the movement of Korean "comfort women" to demand a formal apology from the Japanese government. (Poster Atnine Film 엣나인필름)

The Destruction of Korean Culture and Identity

The Koreans, who remained in their occupied home country, experienced humiliation and physical ill-treatment by the Japanese authority. Japan tried to destroy the Korean identity by eliminating cultural symbols reminiscent of Korea's independent history, that is, the cultural riches of previous Korean kingdoms (Tudor 2012, 38). Japan demolished the main royal palace of the Joseon dynasty in Seoul as well as many other Korean cultural heritage buildings. One of the royal palace buildings, Changgyeong-gung was turned into a zoo and was renamed as Changgyeon-won in 1911 (The Hankyoreh, 1 November 2017). Palace gates such as Doneumun and parts of the Seoul fortress constructions were destroyed. Looting from Korean Buddhist temples, Japan plundered numerous cultural artifacts. Between 1910 and 1916 alone, Japan stole about 18,000 cultural artifacts from Korea (Joe WJ 731:774). The occupying forces tried to eradicate Korean cultural traditions including Korean neo-Confucianism, Buddhism and Korean shamanism. While Korea and Japan adopted Buddhism and Confucianism from China, their understanding and practices of the two philosophies are significantly different. Korean Buddhists became resentful of the introduction of Japanese Buddhist practice, which allowed monks' marriage, in contrast to the Korean tradition of celibacy. In addition, Japan forced its state religion, Shintoism, upon the Koreans. Shintoism requires all of Japan's subjects to worship Japan's emperor as the descendant of the Sun God. Starting from 1935, Japan ordered all Koreans to erect a Shinto shrine at home and forced all Korean teachers and students to worship at Shinto shrines everyday (Oliver 1993: 118-119).

Starting from 1910, Japan banned all Korean newspapers and blacklisted books containing Korean legendary figures such as General Lee Soon-sin who defeated the Japanese navy during the Imjinwaeran in the 16th century. Between 1910 and 1912, the Japanese authority confiscated 200,000 books on Korea's history (Shin CH, 2014) and burnt some 300,000 books that were taken from school libraries and yangban families (Joe WJ 731: 772). As a result, many of the historical documents on Korea's ancient kingdoms were destroyed.

Furthermore, by the late 1930s, Japan outright deprived Koreans of the right to speak and write in their own language. Only the Japanese language was used in schools and the teaching of Korean language and literature was forbidden at all levels of education. As a result, by the end of the Japanese rule, about 70 percent of all Koreans became illiterate in their own language (Oliver, 1993:147). The guiding principle of Japan's education policy in Korea was "to insure a little education (enough to produce a low-skill, low-paid work force) but to discourage and restrict the development of a well-educated intelligentsia that might breed rebellion" (Oliver 1993: 151). As hundreds and thousands of Korean schools and colleges were shut down, most Koreans were forced to remain illiterate and were denied of access to the main venues of occupational mobility. In 1939, only 5.52 percent of

Koreans were attending primary schools, 0.13 percent in secondary schools, and 0.12 percent in vocational schools (Oliver 1993:146).

Japan's cultural policy toward Koreans was not only discriminatory to Koreans in terms of social mobility, but also psychologically damaging and humiliating. Starting from 1939, Japan forced Koreans to change their surname to Japanese names. Instead of Korean family names, such as Kim, Park, and Lee, Koreans had to adopt Japanese names such as Watanabe and Komatzu. The Japanization of Korean surname was "an especially demeaning betrayal of their (Korean) ancestry" (Oliver 1993: 146) and an unbearably shameful act for Koreans who used to worship their ancestors according to their Confucius traditions.

The Korean poetry against the Japanization of Korea

The film, "Dongju: The Portrait of a Poet", is based on the life story of a Korean poet, Yoon Dong-ju (윤 동주 1917-1945). While Yun was a university student in Tokyo, he was arrested for his role in the movement for Korea's Independence. He died in prison, shortly before Korea's liberation from Japan. It is speculated that the Japanese authority might have used him and other prisoners for a biological experiment, causing his death (SBS News, 15 August 2009).

	Released	2016 (film)
	Director / Writer	Lee Joon-ik / Shin Youn-shik
	Cast	Gang Ha-neul, Park Jung-min
	Synopsis	This is a biographical film about the poet, Yoon Dong-ju. Starting with his early life in Gando, Manchuria (China) to his university years in Japan, it follows his interaction with his Korean independence fighters and sheds a critical light on diverse political currents in the movement of Korea's Independence Movement. (Poster © Choi Yong-jin)

One of his well-known poems is "One night I count the stars" that vividly portrays the sorrow of the colonized Koreans. Today, all Korean children learn Yoon's poems at school.

One Night I Count the Stars

The sky that the seasons pass through
is filled with autumn.
I feel as though I can count, without trouble,
all the stars in the depths of autumn.
The reason I cannot now count all
the stars being etched in my heart
one and two at a time,
is that morning comes too soon;
night still remains until tomorrow,
and my youth is not yet spent.
For one star, a memory;
for one star, love;
for one star, loneliness;
for one star, longing;
for one star, a poem;
for one star, Mother. Mother.

Mother, I try calling each star something beautiful: the names of the children I shared a desk with in primary school; the names of the foreign girls, like Pae, Kyung, and Ok; the names of the young women who are already mothers; the names of our poor neighbors, and of the dove, puppy, rabbit, mule, and deer; and the names of poets, like Francis James and Rainer Maria Rilke.

They are all so far away,
like the stars that are infinitely distant.

And Mother,
you are in far northern Manchuria.
Longing for something, I wrote my name
on the hill, where so much starlight has fallen,
and then buried it.

Perhaps the insects drone during the night,
mourning over my shameful name.

But when winter has passed and spring comes even to my star,
to the hill where my name is buried,
the grass, like that growing green over graves
will grow lush and proud.

(translated by Kay Richards)

The poem, "One Night I Count the Stars", has many references to Yoon's own childhood and youthhood. As the poem states, he grew up in Manchuria where many Korean refugees settled down. There, he attended a Christian independent school run by Koreans. Later, he moved to Japan to pursue a post-secondary education since the Japanese authorities suppressed higher learning in Korea. In the poem, Yoon writes "mourning over my shameful name". Here, the passage refers to his Japanized name and the sense of his guilt that he felt toward changing his Korean name to a Japanized one. At that time, for Koreans wishing to study at a university in Japan, it was mandatory to have a Japanese name. In this context, it is understandable why he wrote the passage, "the names of the foreign girls, like Pae, Kyung, and Ok", although "Pae, Kyung, and Ok" are all Korean names.

The Movement for Korea's Independence

While some government officials desperately sought to regain sovereignty by making appeals to foreign powers, the ordinary Korean masses also actively fought for Korea's independence in diverse ways. The movement for Korea's independence included peaceful demonstrations, cultural and educational activities, armed resistance (targeted assassination of Japanese government officials and Korean traitors), and military campaigns against the Japanese forces. A brief summary of the movement of Korea's independence is as follows.

Peaceful Demonstrations

Since the protectorate treaty of 1905, the Japanese forces arrested about 100,000 Koreans for their opposition to the Japanese rule (Joe WJ 2002:778). Despite the political suppression, Koreans organized peaceful street demonstrations to demand Korea's independence. Involving some 2 million Koreans, the peaceful street protests, known as the March First Independent Movement in 1919, swept through Korea and lasted for a year until it was violently crushed by the Japanese authority.

The catalyst for the massive protest movement was the sudden death of King Gojong in January 1919. It was widely believed that Gojong was poisoned by the Japanese. As the whole nation turned into "a cauldron of deep sorrow" and "boiling resentment" toward Japan (Joe WJ 2002: 806), the demonstration spread like wildfire. Even excluding the demonstrations on the village level, (Joe WJ 2002: 818), it was estimated that more than 2 million Koreans took part in over 1500 demonstrations across the country between March and May 1919.

Though it was largely a peaceful demonstration with the public declaration of Korea's Independence, it was brutally crushed by Japan. The Japanese authority massacred hundreds and thousands of peaceful demonstrators and burnt down hundreds of houses, school and church buildings[13]. In one incident, the Japanese authority set fire to a church building, in which 29 Korean Christian protestors were burnt to death (Oliver, 1993:136). The Japanese police killed more than 7,500 protestors, wounded almost 16,000 people, and imprisoned about 47,000 Koreans. Property damage by the Japanese police was extensive. 47 Korean Church buildings and 715 houses were burned down (Joe WJ 2002: p818; Oliver 1993: 125).

---

[13] As in the case with Korea, the people of India under the British colonial rule suffered a similar fate. In 1919, the British authority killed about 1000 Indian people who peacefully protested against the British occupation of India (Shams 2019).

A Resistance: The Yu Gwan-sun Story (항거: 유관순 이야기)

The film, "Resistance: The Yu Gwan-sun Story", depicts the March First Movement of 1919, the biggest peaceful civil disobedience movement in Korea's modern history prior to the 2016 Candlelight Revolution.

	Released	A Resistance: The Yu Gwan-sun Story
	Director	Jo Min-ho (Released in 2019)
	cast	Go Ah-sung as Yu Gwan-sun
	Synopsis	This film shed light on the stories of the imprisoned female protestors including the 16-year old Yu Gwan-sun (유관순). While focusing on the brutal treatment of the Korean protestors in the prison, it portrays solidarity and patriotism among the prisoners. (Poster © Lotte Entertainment).

The film closely follows the historical events of the March 1st Movement and the life story of Yu Gwan-sun, a high school student who was imprisoned for her participation in the Korean Independence Movement.

Despite Japan's bloody suppression of Korea's independence movement, mass demonstrations resurfaced in 1926 and 1929. When Joseon's last king, Sunjong, died on 25 April 1926, Koreans planned a massive demonstration similar to the March First Movement of 1919. The demonstration was scheduled to take place on the day of Sunjong's funeral, but the plan was uncovered by the Japanese police who then quickly arrested hundreds of Korean activists (Oliver 1993:141-142). The Japanese authority also temporarily banned travel to Seoul, so that Korean masses could not converge in the capital to attend the funeral. Despite the heavy surveillance and control by the Japanese, some 200 courageous Korean students managed to take part in the protest, as they shouted, "long live Korean independence!" along the route of the funeral procession and distributed political leaflets stating the declaration of Korea's Independence. The June 10 Demonstration of 1926 ended with the arrest of more than 200 Korean protestors (Lee KB 1984:363).

In the aftermath of the 1926 Demonstration, a series of industrial action and protests including the Gwangju Student Demonstration of 1929 followed. Between 1927 and 1931, Korean activists formed a coalition of Korean activist groups, called "singanhoe" (신간회), that had about 30,000 members with over a hundred branches outside Seoul[14]. Singanhoe coordinated the organizing efforts toward students and workers (Lee KB 1984: 363).

The Singanhoe's organizing efforts were instrumental in building a mass protest movement, known as the 1929 Gwangju Student Movement, that involved 194 schools and some 54,000 students (Oliver 1993:142). The trigger of the 1929 Gwangju Student Movement was an ill-treatment of Koreans by Japanese residents in Korea. When some Japanese male students threw verbal insults at three Korean female students at a train station in Gwangju, some outraged Korean by-standers clashed with the Japanese students. The student brawl developed into a large-scale street fighting between Koreans and Japanese. When the Japanese police arrested some 400 Korean students and other participants, the entire city of Gwangju erupted in mass protests calling for the release of the imprisoned students and the "abolition of racial discrimination and the overthrow of imperialism". Korean students in other cities took part in solidarity demonstrations that soon spread across the country, involving 194 schools and some 54,000 students. The demonstrations, which continued until 1930, eventually ended with the expulsion of more than 580 students, the suspension of 2,330 students and the imprisonment of over 1,640 people (Lee KB 1984: 364).

As the Japanese forces brutally killed or imprisoned hundreds and thousands of Koreans, many fled the country and set up overseas organizations dedicated to regaining Korea's sovereignty. Some Koreans turned to guerilla warfare, while others looked to an educational campaign to realize the goal. The Korean mass protests and other activities for Korea's Independence served as a catalyst for the emergence of the armed struggle, led by the Korean Provisional Government in exile and numerous resistance groups abroad.

---

[14] Korean activists including the members of the Chosun Communist Party and Chondogyo (the religion based on the teachings of the Donghak movement) established a coalition organization called singanhoe (신간회) and its parallel women's organization, Keunuh-hyeo (근우회) (Lee KB 1984:363).

Released in 1959, the film, "Nameless Stars" deals with the Gwangju student movement for Korea's independence in 1929.

	Title	Nameless Stars (이름없는 별들)
	Released	1959 (Directed by Kim Gang-yun)
	cast	Hwang Hae-nam, Jo Mi-ryeong
	Synopsis	This film sheds light on Seongjinheo (성진회), a clandestine organization, that played a significant role in organizing students' protests against the Japanese rule in Gwangju. (Poster © Korean Film Archive).

The Armed Movement for Korea's Independence

Many Koreans took up arms to fight against the Japanese forces in Korea. Eubyeong (the Righteous Army) was the earliest organization that carried out the armed resistance, including bombing police buildings and assassinating Japanese military officials and Korean traitors. In 1909, An Joong-geun, a member of the Righteous Army (eubyeong), successfully assassinated Ito Hirobumi, the mastermind of Japan's annexation of Korea.

An Joong-Geun

Several movies tell stories about An Joong-geun, one of the most well-known Korean activists who fought against the Japanese colonization of Korea. They include: "King Gojong and Matyr An Joong-geun (고종황제와 안중근 의사)", "Thomas An Joong-geun (도마 안중근)", and "The Righteous Army: The Age of Heroes (의병)". In addition, the musical, "Hero (영웅)", also portrays the life of An.

116

	Title	Thomas An Joong-geun
	Released	2004
	Director	Seo Se-won
	cast	Yu Oh-sung
	Synopsis	The film focuses on An Joong-geun's role in the Korean armed resistance movement against Japan (Poster © SourceOne Production).

An Joong-geun (1879-1910) assassinated Ito Hirobumi in 1909 at the Harbin railroad station in China. He was executed in a Japanese prison in 1910 (Han 1995).

About 142,000 people belonged to the Righteous Army (eubyeong) and they mounted numerous armed assaults on the Japanese military throughout the late 1800s and early 1900s (Oliver 1993: 98). The poorly equipped eubyeong, however, took a heavy blow from the Japanese military responses, as the Japanese authority hunted down the Righteous Army. The Japanese army killed about 18,000 Korean eubyeong members and wounded about 3,700 as of 1912 (Oliver 1993: 98). In this context, many of the remaining members of eubyeong moved to China or Russia to continue their struggle.

The Righteous Army (Eubyeong)

Most K-dramas and movies on the fall of Joseon contain some scenes or references to the activities of the Righteous Army. For instance, the TV drama, "Mr. Sunshine", tells the stories of the Righteous Army that included Koreans from all walks of life including farmers and members of aristocratic yangban families.

Scheduled to be released in 2019, the TV series, "The Righteous Army: The Age of heroes" (의군: 푸른 영웅의 시대), provides a spotlight on the workings of Eubyeong with a focus on An Jung-geun.

Righteous army in 1907. The man in a black uniform is a soldier from the disbanded Korean Army. (Photo by F.A. McKenzie. Public Domain)

Korean activists set up military schools or military training centres in Manchuria (China) and Siberia (Russia) (Joe WJ 2002: 819). One of the most famous military training camp was the Sinheung Military School (신흥무관학교) in Manchuria. With more than one million Korean refugees in Manchuria, the region provided a natural base for Korean armed resistance groups. Although on a smaller scale, Korean military training camps existed even in Hawaii and Nebraska in the USA, where some Korean migrants lived in the early 1900s[15]. Already, in 1909, Park Yong-man (박 용만) operated the Military Academy for Korean Boys (한인소년병학교) in Nebraska. He later set up the Military School for the People of Great Joseon (대조선 국민군단병 학교)[16] in Hawaii in 1912 (Yonhap News, 26 February 2019).

---

[15] Hundreds and thousands of Koreans emigrated to the USA in the early 1900s, as the country needed foreign workers for the construction of railway (Nebraska) and the cultivation of sugar plantations (Hawaii).

[16] The military school was shut down by the US authority in 1915, mainly due to Rhee Seung-man's sectarian sabotage against Park Yong-man who was actively

In the wake of the March First Movement of 1919, organizations of independence fighters grew in number. In the 1920s, more than thirty organizations were actively engaged in armed struggles against the Japanese army in Manchuria (China) and Siberia (Russia) (KOCIS 2019). Some notable armed resistance groups included the Euyeoldan (Righteous Heroes Unit), the Aeguktan (Patriotic Unit), the Hanguk Independence Army and the Joseon Independence Army (Pratt and Rutt 1999: 186). On numerous occasions, the Korean independence fighters mounted attacks on the units of the Japanese military and police forces not only in Korea but also in China (Lee KB 1984:364). Some well-known battles led by Korean fighters include the battles of Bongoh-dong, Chongsan-ni, and Daejeonjaryong that took place between the 1920s and 1930s.

The Bongohdong Battle (봉오동 전투)

The Bongohdong Battle, which took place in Manchuria in June 1920, ended with the first large scale military victory for Korean independence fighters. More than 150 Japanese soldiers perished in the battle, while over 200 were severely injured.

	Title	The Battle: Roar to Victory
	Production	2019
	Cast	Yu Hae-jin, Ryu Joon-yeol
	Synopsis	The film tells the story about how Korean freedom fighters cornered the numerically and militarily superior Japanese troops into a deadly trap and ultimately led the battle to the victory for Koreans. (Poster Big Stone Pictures/ Showbox)

---

involved in training Korean fighters. Disagreeing with Park's military strategy, Rhee only advocated for a peaceful and diplomatic solution for Korea's independence (Yonhap News, 26 February 2019).

In 1920, the Korean fighters of the Northern Route Military Unit (북로군정서), led by Kim Jwa-jin, inflicted a heavy blow on the Japanese army by killing more than 1000 Japanese soldiers. The military conflict is known as Chungsan-ri battle. In retaliation, the Japanese Army slaughtered hundreds of Korean civilians and burnt down several Korean settlements in Manchuria (Lee KB 1984:365).

Although millions of Koreans fled their homeland to escape political persecution and economic hardship under the Japanese rule, they continued their efforts to restore Korea's independence from abroad. To this end, the overseas Koreans established the Provisional Government of Korea (PGK). By 1919, several organizations proclaimed to be a provisional government of independent Korea. They included the Provisional Government of Joseon (조선민국임시정부), the Provisional Government of the New Korea (신한민국임시정부), the Government of the Great Han People (대한민간정부), the Republican Government of Goryeo (고려공화정부), the Provisional Government of Korea in Gando (간도임시정부), and the Provisional Government of Korea in Shanghai (상해임시정부). Among them, only a few organizations had a sizable membership and a significant support base (Kim SU, 2019). The Provisional Government of Korea in Shanghai was the most influential organization of all.

* The Provisional Government of Korea in Shanghai

The Provisional Government of Korea in Shanghai was established in April 1919. The PGK adopted a democratic constitution that proclaimed Korea as a democratic republic as opposed to a traditional monarchy. The Constitution of PGK outlined a political system based on popular sovereignty (electoral rights for the general populace) and the separation of three branches of state power (executive, legislative and judicial) (KOCIS 2019).

The Provisional Government of Korea in exile (PGK) included Korean activists with divergent political ideas. Disagreeing on political strategies, the members of the PGK argued over the political direction and tactics of the PGK. The first president of PGK, Rhee Seung-man, preferred a diplomatic approach, focusing on winning support from the major Atlantic powers. Other leaders of PGK such as Yi Tong-hui emphasized guerrilla warfare and the necessity to organize Korean fighters into formidable military forces.

They were also willing to work with Chinese or Russian counterparts against the Japanese army. Some Korean activists such as An Chang-ho preferred the educational movement as the main focus of the PGK activity (Oliver 1993). In an ideal world, the PGK would have carried out every campaign that might have helped Korean endeavour to regain sovereignty. In reality, however, the PGK was constrained by limited resources and thus, the leaders of the PGK bitterly argued over political priorities of the PGK as to how their limited resources should be used.

Photo 5.1 The Provisional Government of Korea in Shanghai (Public Domain)

The early PGK leadership was heavily dominated by pro-American Koreans such as Rhee Seung-man who denounced the Korean armed struggle and instead stressed only a diplomatic approach to gain support from foreign governments (especially the USA). Rhee's diplomatic success with the major Atlantic powers did not materialize. Resentment and disputes grew within the PGK, as Rhee and his pro-Western activists spent the limited resources of the PGK by travelling around the world to make a futile appeal to the American government and the League of Nations. In 1920, on behalf of the Provisional Government in exile, Rhee tried to appeal to the League of Nations, but the Korean delegates were denied of entry.

The principle of national self-determination, advocated by the American president Woodrow Wilson, was apparently meant for only the former colonies of the defeated Germany. In other words, the colonies of the victorious allies including the USA, Britain and Japan were denied of the right to self-determination (Oliver, 1993:126). Rhee pleaded the American Department of State to give Koreans a chance to speak at the Peace Conference. Rejecting Rhee's plea, the State Department said: "In view of the fact that the US has recognized the annexation of Korea, the representative ought not to be received" (Oliver 1993: 139). When Rhee pointed out that the American response was "a denial of every principle" and asked whether "the American government will be able to do anything in regard to giving the Koreans a hearing", he received no reply (Oliver 1993:139).

The Provisional Government of Korea in Exile

Several TV series dramas and films depict the activities of the PGK. They include: "Different Dreams", "Assassination", and "Shanghai Provisional Government" (상해 임시정부).

	Title	Shanghai Provisional Government
	Production	1969 (Directed by Jo Geung-ha)
	Cast	Shin Seong-il, Kim Ji-mi
	Synopsis	The film focuses on the role of Kim Gu in the Provisional Government of Korea in Shanghai. (Poster Daeyang Film Production)

While residing in the USA, Rhee continued to make fruitless efforts to have the Korean claims reviewed by the Disarmament Conference in Washington in 1921-22. Without consulting with the Provisional Government, Rhee even proposed that Korea should be under the trusteeship of the United Nation.

After numerous arguments between Rhee and other PGK leaders, Lee Dong-hui and An Chang-ho resigned from the PGK. In 1925, Rhee was impeached by the Provisional Government on a charge of neglecting his presidential duties (Oliver 1993: 141). After Rhee Seung-man and his elitist supporters alienated many freedom fighters, the PGK leadership eventually moved from Rhee to Kim Gu who did not reject a guerrilla warfare as part of the independence movement.

The PGK came under the leadership of Kim Gu. Kim Gu established the Korean Independence Party (한국독립당) in 1930. Under Kim Gu's leadership, the party carried out numerous military missions against Japan, including its attempt to assassinate the Japanese emperor in 1932 (Pratt and Rutt 1999: 236). Kim Gu organized Acguktan (Patriotic Corps), a secret guerilla unit, as part of the PGK's armed forces (Oliver 1993: 141). Through Aeguktan, the PGK carried out many military missions against the Japanese authority. For instance, Yoon Bong-gil (1908-1932, a member of Aeguktan), detonated a bomb at a gathering of Japanese officials in Shanghai, killing many high-ranking Japanese military officials in April 1932 (Lee KB 1984:366).

The Korean Armed Resistance Movement	
This film, "Assassination" (암살), depicts the life of guerrilla fighters working for the Provisional Government of Korea in Shanghai.	
Title	Assassination (암살)
Released	2015 (Directed by Choi Dong-hoon)
Cast	Jeon Ji-hyun, Lee Jung-jae, Ha Jung-woo
Synopsis	Set in the 1930s, the Provisional Government of Korea sends An Ok-Yoon, a deadly sniper, on a mission to assassinate a Japanese general in Korea. A traitor (Yem Sek-jin) informs the Japanese authority and they try to foil the assassination plot. (Poster © Caper film)

Most characters in the film, except a few people (e.g. Hawaii Pistol), are modelled after real historical figures. They are as follows.

Ahn Ok-gyun, the female sniper: The main character, An Ok-yoon, is modelled after Nam Ja-hyeon (1872-1933) who was a guerilla fighter in Manchuria. After the failure of the 1919 March First Movement, in which she took part, she fled the country from the Japanese persecution of Korean activists and joined an armed resistance group in Manchuria. Later, she returned to Korea on a secret mission to assassinate Japanese Admiral Saito Makoto. Largely borrowing from the biographical elements of Nam Ja-hyeon, the film dramatizes the assassin by adding some fictional stories about her family background.

General Kim Jwa-jin and the Chungsanri Battle in 1920: In the film, An Ok-gyun bitterly recollects the Gando massacre whereby over 3000 Koreans were brutally killed by the Japanese military as a retaliation of its defeat in the Chungsanri battle. The Chungsanri battle and the massacre really took place in 1920. An armed resistance group, the North Route Army of Korea, led by General Kim Jwa-jin, defeated the Japanese army in the battle of Chungsan-ri that resulted in more than 3000 casualties. In retaliation, the Japanese military savagely massacred thousands of Korean refugees over two months in several villages of Manchuria. The massacre is known as "gyeongsin chambyeon" (The massacre in the year of gyeongsin).

In addition to Aegookdan, numerous armed resistance groups fought against the Japanese forces in and around Korea. To name a few, they included: the Northern Route Army (북로정서군), the Korea Independence Army (대한독립군), the Korea Liberation Army (대한광복군), Euyoldan (Righteous Brotherhood 의열단), the Korean People's Revolutionary Army (KPRA), Eugoonbu (의군부), Bokhwangdan (복황단), Changeudan (창의단), Daehan Sinmindan (대한신민단), Hyeolsungdan (혈성단), the New Korean Youth (신대한 청년회), the Youth Wild Tiger (청년 맹호단), the Student Group for the Restauration of Korean Sovereignty (학생광복단), and Jawidan (자위단) (Kim SU, 2019a).

Among the armed resistance groups, Kim Wonbong's Euyoldan (Righteous Brotherhood) is the most famous one. Euyeoldan had about 1000 members throughout Korea and its neighboring areas including Manchuria and Siberia. It later developed into the Righteous Army of Joseon (Joseon Euyongdae 조선의용대) in 1938 (Kim SU, 2019b).

Dramas on the Armed Resistance Groups

The TV series, "Different Dreams", shed light on the life of Kim Won-bong (1898-1958) and the activities of his guerrilla group, Euyoldan. It also depicts other Korean freedom fighters, with a focus on Aegukdan (Patriots' Group) under the Provisional Government of Korea in Shanghai. Initially, the PGK was reluctant to collaborate with Korean guerilla groups but later changed its approach by collaborating closely with Kim Won-bong's Euyoldan.

	Title	Different Dreams (이 몽)
	Aired	2019 (TV series)
	cast	Yoo Ji-tae, Lee Yo-won
	Synopsis	The drama tells a story about Kim Won-bong, the leader of Euyoldan, and Lee Yong-jin, a female doctor, who secretly works for the Provisional Government of Korea, under the leadership of Kim Gu. (Poster © MBC)

Aside from Kim Won-bong, the drama sheds light on numerous Korean freedom fighters including, Lee Tae-joon (1883-1921), Kim Sang-ok (1890-1923), Park Esther (1876-1910), Park Cha-jeong (1910-1944), and Jeong Jeong-hwa (1900-1991).

The drama has slightly changed the names of real activists, as it spices up historical events with fictional ones. In the drama, Kim Sang-ok (1890-1923) appears as Kim Nam-ok, and Lee Tae-joon (1883-1921) as Yoo Tae-joon. Each episode ends with an ending credit that shows the real names of Korean fighters who were the models for fictional figures in the drama. Some notable historical events that the drama had references to are as follows.

The drama features Lee Tae-joon (1883-1921), a Korean doctor and a Korea independence fighter. The drama begins with Kim Won-bong seeking the whereabouts of Yoo Tae-Joon (real name Lee Tae-joon) who was responsible for delivering the support funds from the Russian government. This is referenced to the real historical events surrounding the political funds given by the Soviet government under Lenin. The Bolshevik government in Russia provided 400,000 Ruble (in the form of gold bars), to be used for the Korean independence movement. The challenge was to safely deliver the funds across Russia and China where some areas were in control of anti-Bolshevik forces including the ultra-rightist Russians and the Japanese military. Thus, the funds were divided into several portions and a secret delivery mission was assigned to a few Korean activists including Lee Tae-joon. Serving as a liaison between the Soviets and the Korean independence groups, Lee Ta-joon was not only a leading Korean activist but also a medical doctor who worked in Mongolia at that time. In 1921, he was killed by the Russian White Army that controlled some parts of Russia and Mongolia against the Soviet government during the Russian Civil War (1917-23).

Other resistance groups such as Kim Gu's Aegukdan and the Korean People's Revolutionary Army (KPRA), the military wing of the Korean Revolutionary Party in Manchuria, were actively engaged in military campaigns against the Japanese military throughout the 1930s and the early 1940s (Pratt and Rutt 1999: 238).

The PGK under Kim Gu largely worked with divergent independence groups in China and Russia, such as Kim Won-bong's Euyoldan. In 1940, the PGK organized the Korean Liberation Army (Gwangbokgun), headquartered in Chungqing (China), and dispatched its military units to fight on the side of the Allied Forces during WWII (KOCIS 2019). In 1944, various independence organizations across a broad political spectrum agreed to work under the leadership of the PGK. The coalition within the PGK included the Party for Korea's Independence (한국독립당), the Revolutionary Party of Joseon Nation (조선민족혁명당), the Alliance for Joseon's Liberation (조선민족해방동맹), and the League of the Joseon Anarchists (조선무정부주의자 총연맹) (Kim SU, 2019a).

The Cultural Movement for Korea's Independence

Many Korean activists turned to mass education based on patriotic programs as a means to resist the Japanization of Korea. An Chang-ho (1878-1938) and Yi Tong Hui, both leading members of the PGK, helped to build some 170 independent schools in the northern part of Korea and 73 in Ganghwa (Joe, WJ 2000:722). Pak Eun-sik (1859-1925), the second president of the PGK, established night schools designed for workers. Most independent schools were on the middle school level, with students aged in their 20s or 30s. The Korean schools taught modern subjects as opposed to neo-Confucian classics. The school routine also included some physical training and the singing of the Korean national anthem and other patriotic songs (Joe, WJ 2000: 724). Korean refugees in China and Russia also voluntarily set up independent Korean schools to teach their children. As of 1908, Vladivostok and other Russian towns had 11 Korean schools, while more than 130 independent schools existed in China's Gando by 1910 (Joe, WJ 2000:723).

MAL • MO • E: The Secret Mission (말모이)

The film, "Mal mo e", sheds light on the Korean Language Society (조선어학회), a clandestine organization that tried to produce a comprehensive Korean language dictionary. The film title, "Mal mo-e," means "to collect vocabulary" in Korean.

	Title	MAL • MO • E: The Secret Mission
	Released	2019 (Director: Eom Yu-na)
	Cast	Yoo Hae-jin, Yoon Kye-sang
	Synopsis	Kim Pan-Soo, an illiterate single-father, encounters a group of Korean scholars who are secretly working toward the publication of a first comprehensive Korean dictionary. Under the Japanese surveillance, the Korean scholars face numerous obstacles and danger. Kim helps out the scholars, first out of economic necessities but later out of his own volition, as he learns the cultural importance of Korean language for his children. (Poster © Lotte Culture Works)

By dramatizing the real historical events involving the Korean Language Society, this film sheds a critical light on Japan's brutal policy of cultural assimilation that aimed to eliminate Korean identity. The main character in the film, Rye Jung-hwan, is based on the real historical figure, Lee Geuk-roh (1893-1978). After returning from his study at Humboldt University in Germany, he declined offers for prestigious and well-paid positions and instead dedicated his life to the preservation of Korean language. In 1929, he organized the Korean Language Society and began collecting all Korean words including dialects. By 1942, when his organization almost completed the compilation work, the Japanese police arrested the group members and confiscated their work. Including Lee, 33 members of the Korean Language Society were imprisoned and were brutally tortured. They were released from the prison only after Korea was liberated from Japan in 1945. He resumed the previous work of compiling Korean vocabulary and published the first Korean dictionary in 1947.

The film contains some fictional elements. Kim Pan-soo and his two children in the film are fictional figures. The main character's father is portrayed as a school director who collaborated with the Japanese authority. In reality, however, the father of Lee Geuk-roh (이극로) was an ordinary farmer and did not support the Japanese rule.

As for Koreans under the Japanese occupation, they secretly ran societies and groups that published Korean literature, newspapers and periodicals in defiance of Japanese repressive cultural policy. Koreans made sustained efforts to promote the use of Korean language and tried to preserve traditional Korean music and literature (Pratt and Rutt 1999: 82).

Divergent Paths to Korea's Independence

The Korean Independence Movement consisted of diverse political parties, guerrilla units, and various clandestine organizations, all dedicated to the restoration of Korean sovereignty. For instance, they included: the Korean

Communist Party (KCP) or the Chosun Communist Party (조선공산당)[17], Korean People's Revolutionary Army (KPRA), the Korean Independence Party (한국독립당), the Korean People's Socialist Party (KPSP)[18], the Koryo Communist Party (고려공산당)[19], Sinheung Military Academy (신흥무관학교), Sinhan Youth Party (신한청년당), Euyeoldan (의열단), the Joseon Revolutionary Party (조선혁명당), the League of Joseon Anarchists (조선무정부주의자연맹), the League of Joseon National Front (조선민족전선연맹), the League of Joseon Independence (조선독립연맹), Daehan Independence Group (대한독립단), the Goryeo Revolutionary Party (고려혁명당), Gyeongsung Communist Group (경성코뮤니스트그룹), the Group of Korean Patriots (한인애국단), the New People's Association (신민회)[20], Restoration Association (광복회), Korean People's Association (국민회), and the Korean Women's Patriotic Association (대한민국애국부인회). Many of the political parties and groups worked together under the Provisional Government of Korea in exile, although their co-operation was often punctuated with factional fights and internal rivalry stemming from their political differences. In 1944, most major political groupings including the leftist decided to work together under the umbrella of the PGK.

Korean leftists played a significant role in the Korean Independence Movement. Since the 1917 Bolshevik Revolution in Russia, many Koreans favorably viewed communist movements. Russia came to help the Korean Independence Movement since the 1917 Bolshevik revolution that established a workers' government based on the collective ownership of property and a planned economy. Advocating international workers' solidarity against imperialism, the Russian Bolshevik government under Lenin called for the emancipation of all colonized countries around the world.

---

[17] The Korean Communist Party (KCP) or Chosun Communist Party (조선공산당) was established in 1925 by Jo Bong-am and Park Heon-young. The KCP had about 680,000 members in 1947 (Pratt and Rutt 1999: 233).

[18] The Korean People's Socialist Party (KPSP) was formed by Lee Dong-hui in 1918. Based in Siberia, the KPSP received some help from the Bolshevik government of Russia.

[19] The Goryo Communist Party was formed in Shanghai in 1920.

[20] The New People's Association (Shinmheo 신민회) was established in 1907 by An Chang-ho and Lee Dong-nyeong. In 1911, the Japanese authority arrested 600 Korean activists including many members of Shinminheo group (Lee HE, 1995).

Toward this goal, the Russian government financed anti-colonial endeavours worldwide, including the Korean movement for independence. In this context, Koreans, deeply inspired by the Bolshevik revolution that proclaimed its goal for an egalitarian society free from colonial subjugation and exploitation by large landowners, joined various leftist organizations. In stark contrast to Russia under the Bolshevik government, the governments of the Atlantic Powers showed little interest in Korean pleas for independence and instead publicly supported Japan's domination over Korea. Seen from this historical hindsight, it is not surprising that many Korean freedom fighters at that time were either communists or at least very sympathetic to the international communist movement.

Independence Fighters Across the Political Spectrum

Historical memories are selective. The ideology of incumbent power holders greatly shapes historical narratives. As far as South Korea is concerned, the role of leftist forces in Korea's independence movement is largely ignored or negatively portrayed in its official historical narratives. This omission or distortion is often reflected in the contents of K-dramas and films. Deviating from this trend, some recent films shed positive light on the role of leftist activists in the resistance movement.

	Title	Anarchist from Colony
	Production	Directed by Lee Joon-ik (2017)
	Cast	Lee Je-hoon, Choi Hee-seo
	Synopsis	Park Yeol was a member of "Bulryeongsa", the anarchist group, that plotted an attempt to assassinate Japanese government officials. This film focuses on the real life story of Park Yeol. (Poster © Megabox Plus M)

The film, "Park Yeol", shed light on Korean anarchists in Japan and the massacre of Koreans in the aftermath of the Kanto earthquake in 1923. Albeit in small numbers, some Korean anarchists contributed to the Korea independence movement in Japan in the 1920s. One of the Korean anarchists, Park Yeol, was imprisoned for plotting a plan to assassinate

---

> the Japanese emperor (Lee KB 1984:361). The film is based on the true story of the Korean anarchist, Park Yeol (1902-1974), who fought for Korea's independence in Japan.

Russian and Chinese Support for Korea's Independence Movement

The funding for Korea's Independence Movement including the PGK mainly came from donations of ordinary Korean workers and farmers. In addition, being hostile to Japan, the Russian government under Lenin and the Chinese government under the Kuomintang, came to help Korea. As for Russia, Lee Tong-hui, a leading member of PGK and the founder of the Korean People's Socialist Party, asked the Bolshevik government of Russia for financial support and military supplies for Korean groups in Manchuria and Siberia. The Soviet government provided 600,000 rubles, with a promise of a total of 2 million (Oliver, 1993:140).

As in the case with Russia, China's Kuomintang led by Chiang Kai-suk provided some help to the PGK. In the 1930s, some Korean activists received military training at the Chinese Military Academy (Pratt and Rutt 1999: 186). When China's Manchuria came under Japanese control, Korean guerrillas joined with Chinese militias to fight against Japan's puppet government in Manchuria (Lee KB 1984:365). With Japan's conquest of Manchuria in the 1930s, the organized recruitment and training of Korean troops moved to Siberia and elsewhere. Under the protection of the Bolshevik government of Russia, Siberia provided a new training ground to tens and thousands of Korean leftists and the Korean Independence Army (Oliver 1993: 141).

It should be noted that at the end of WWII, the US government refused to acknowledge the PGK as the legitimate government of Korea. Instead, Washington chose Rhee Seung-man (the impeached former PGK president) and his right-wing supporters as the legitimate Korean representatives who could work with the American military government in the South (Kim SU, 2019b).

TV series and Films on Korea's Colonial History

Between 1910 and 1945, Japan ruled Korea in an extremely brutal manner. Even today, the memories of Japanese atrocities against Koreans still evoke a strong sentiment of indignation and outrage among the Korean people. Korean national identity has been deeply influenced by the collective memories of the Korean suffering at the hands of the Japanese occupation forces, as well as by the memories of the Korean Independence movement. Such memories of the collective suffering and the collective resistance have served as a catalyst for "the soul of a nation" (Renan) or the "conscience collective" (Durkheim). As Renan put it, the soul of a nation lives on the shared memories of "collective suffering, sacrifice, and national heroes". Historical TV dramas and films dealing with the Japanese occupation of Korea are full of such themes that highlight the collective suffering of Koreans and the sacrifices borne by Korean freedom fighters.

K-Dramas and films on Colonized Korea

Since the democratization of South Korea in the early 1990s, numerous films and TV series dramas have been produced to shed light on the Japanese atrocities and the heroic resistance of the Korean people against the Japanese occupation of Korea.

Table 5.1 TV series and films on Korea under the Japanese occupation

Assassination (암살), Prince Deokhye (덕혜옹주), Thomas An Joong-geun (도마 안중근), Spirits Coming (귀향), The Battleship Island (군함도), Dong-ju (동주), The Age of Shadow (밀정), Anarchist from Colony (Park Yeol), Bridal Mask (각시탈), Praise of Death (사의찬미), Capital Scandal, Anarchist (아나키스트), Freedom Fighter, Lee Hoe-young (자유인 이회영), Different Dreams (이몽), Inspiring Generation (감격시대), YMCA Baseball Team (YMCA 야구단), The Good, the Bad, the Weird (좋은 놈, 나쁜 놈, 이상한 놈), The Last Comfort Women (마지막 위안부), A Resistance: The Story of Yoo Gwan-sun (항거: 유관순 이야기), Tuning Fork (소리굽쇠), The Eyes of Dawn (여명의 눈), Journal of Baekbeom (백범일지), War and Peace (전쟁과 사랑), Mimang (미망), The Righteous Army: The Age of Heroes (의군: 푸른 영웅의 시대), Yu Gwan-sun (유관순), and "1919 Yu Gwan-sun (1919 유관순).

Released in 2010, the TV drama, "Freedom Fighter, Lee Hoe-yeong," depicts the life of Lee Hoe-yeong, a Korean independence fighter. He set up a military school in Manchuria to train Koreans to fight against the Japanese forces. Some TV series tell mostly fictional stories of imaginary Korean fighters. For instance, released in 2014, the TV series, "Inspiring Generation", depict the story of Korean independence fighters in Shanghai in the 1930s. Unlike many historical TV dramas, this drama is not based on real historical figures. Similarly, "Capital Scandal" (TV series), based on a novel, tells a story of a Korean playboy who falls in love with a Korean freedom fighter.

Although many TV drama series and films depicting Korean activists are available, they are largely biased against leftist activists, as South Korean TV dramas tend to underplay the leftist contribution to the Korean Independence movement. The Cold War ideology, the Korean War and the subsequent division of Korea, all heavily influenced the ways in which South Koreans understand the politics of the Korea Independence Movement.

As many TV series dramas and films dealing with Korea's colonial history clearly demonstrate, Koreans under the Japanese rule were subjected to tremendous humiliation and indescribably brutal treatment. This collective suffering at the hands of the Japanese is still remembered by Koreans today. Especially, in the absence of apologies from the Japanese government, the cruel Japanese atrocities during the colonial period still provoke strong sentiments of anger and resentment among Koreans. True reconciliation, at the level of the citizenry, is highly unlikely, as long as the Japanese government under the conservative Liberal Democratic Party refuses to acknowledge Japan's violent colonial history by denying or whitewashing the Imperial Japan's crimes against Koreans.

Chapter 6

The Division of Korea

On 6 August 1945, the USA dropped the first nuclear bomb on Hiroshima. Three days later, it dropped the second atomic bomb on Nagasaki. Afterwards, Japan surrendered unconditionally. With Japan's surrender, WWII in Asia finally ended, while the war in Europe had already ended earlier with the defeat of Germany in May 1945. With Japan's defeat, Korea was finally liberated from the Japanese rule in 1945. Korea was, however, divided into North and South and came under the Soviet and American occupation (1945-1948) respectively. The Cold War geopolitics surrounding the Korean peninsula and the inter-Korean conflicts since 1948 eventually led to the Korean Civil War (1950-1953). This chapter gives an overview of the international as well as domestic political context of Korea's division during the period between 1945 and 1953.

The Geopolitical Context

By the late 1930s, the configuration of international power rivalry took a major shift. As Japan expanded its control over many Asian countries, it clashed with other colonial powers in the region, including Japan's former allies, Britain and the USA. Due to conflicting geopolitical interests in Asia, Japan broke off its relations with the USA and Britain. In December 1941, Japan launched a surprise military attack on Pearl Harbor in Hawaii that was an American colony. With the USA joining World War II, the American foreign policy toward Korea changed from being an indifferent accomplice to a stakeholder. In this context, the USA took a greater interest in the fate of Korea and other Asian colonies of Japan.

No colonial powers, both the old and the new, had voluntarily given up their colonies. Major colonial powers in Asia such as Great Britain, France and the USA did not want to grant full independence to their colonies (such as Vietnam, Indonesia, Malaysia, Burma, etc.) even after the end of WWII. If they appear to grant independence to their colonies, it is because they had already prepared a political arrangement to ensure their geopolitical interests in their former-colonies. The American and European colonial powers engineered various political arrangements short of full independence for their own colonies and the former colonies of the defeated Japan and Germany. They pushed forward a trusteeship of colonies. Trusteeship meant a period of political supervision by foreign powers before independence, so that the trustees could ensure a desirable regime change.

Already in 1943, the Allied Forces of WWII had made a multipower trusteeship plan for Japan's colonies including Korea. In April 1943, the USA and Great Britain worked out a proposal for an international trusteeship program for Korea. According to the proposal, Korea would be put under a 40-year trusteeship (Oliver, 1993:157-158). The trusteeship plan for Korea changed several times since 1943, as American geopolitical relationship with Russia and China shifted from being a cautious collaborator to a hostile rival.

Toward the end of WWII, the old trusteeship plan for Korea was replaced by a new plan of trusteeship for the duration of 5 years, this time under a joint control of only the two superpowers, the Soviet Union and the USA. While Washington did not want to allow Russia a role in shaping the future of Japan, it accepted a compromising solution toward Korea (Oliver, 1993:197). Therefore, the two parties agreed to a power-sharing plan that would divide Korea into two zones, one under the American and the other under the Soviet. In September 1945, Korea was put under Soviet and American occupation. A few months later, however, a different trusteeship plan was drawn up. In December 1945, representatives of the USA, Britain, and the Soviet Union met in Moscow and revised the plan for Korea. They agreed to a four-power trusteeship for Korea for five years, which would be administered jointly by four powers, the Soviets, the US, Great Britain, and China (Oliver, 1993:166).

By 1947, the Cold War between the United States and the Soviet Union, began to set in. Eastern Europe fell under the influence of the Soviets. In addition, mainland China came under the rule of communists in 1949. Facing the expanding bloc of communist regimes, the American government calculated that American geo-political interests would be better served by maintaining South Korea as a bulwark against the communist bloc in Asia (Oliver, 1993:178). Consequently, in 1948, Washington abandoned the four-power trusteeship program and abrogated the 1945 Moscow agreement despite Russian objection. The US instead proposed that the issue of Korea should be decided by the United Nations (UN).

Immediately after WWII, the USA emerged as the global superpower, since it held enormous economic (the largest economy in the world) and military power (its monopoly of the atomic bomb). Using its economic wealth to provide international aid and loans to countries devastated by the war, the USA exerted its political influence on most countries outside of the Soviet bloc. In this context, the USA established the United Nations in October 1945 as the successor of the ineffective League of Nations. Although the UN was supposed to be a multilateral inter-state body for global governance, it was back then de facto an organization that largely functioned as a rubber stamp for American foreign policies. With the membership of 50 countries, closely allied with the USA, the inter-state organization of the UN largely held a favorable view toward American foreign policies. As the historian Oliver put it, "Except the veto power of the Security Council members (China, Russia, Britain, France, and the US), the US enjoyed a virtual 'automatic majority' in the UN. When the US requested that the UN take on the Korean problem, acceptance of the request was inevitable" (Oliver, 1993:198).

At the UN meetings, the US and the Soviets proposed different solutions. The Soviets proposed that all foreign troops be withdrawn from Korea by the beginning of 1948. According to the American proposal, separate elections should be held under the sponsorship of the occupation forces, with observation by the UN and the National Assembly (with the more populous South Korea having two-thirds of the Assembly membership) would decide the constitution of the united Korea (Oliver, 1993:199). Without consulting with Koreans, the UN supported the American proposal for the separate elections (Oliver, 1993:196) and paved the way for the creation of two separate states: the Democratic People's Republic of Korea (North Korea) and the Republic of Korea (South Korea).

North Korea under the Soviet Occupation (1945-1948)

After Korea was liberated from Japan, about 35,000 Korean Communists in Siberia, the largest organized Korean exiled group in Asia, returned to Korea. With the return of other Korean independence groups from China and elsewhere, they began organizing Korean grass-root organizations such as People's Committees.

As for leftist Koreans who fought against the Japanese rule, they belonged to one of the three main communist camps: the domestic Koreans (Korean Communist Party led by Park Heon-young), the Yenan-Koreans (the New People's Party led by Kim Du-bong), and the Siberian-Koreans (the North Korean Labor Party led by Kim Il-sung), among many others. While the Soviet occupation forces worked with the local Korean groups, they favored the Siberian Koreans due to their close ties in many respects. First of all, there was no language barrier between the Siberian communist group and the Russians. Secondly, the Siberian-Koreans were politically closer to the Russian communists than to the Chinese.

Among the leftist forces in the North, the Siberian communist faction led by Kim Il-sung[21] came to dominate the transitional government in the North under the Soviet occupation. Russian forces favored Kim not only because he was fluent in Russian but also because he served as a major in the Soviet Army. In this context, Kim Il-sung was appointed by the Soviet to the position of power in charge of the transitional government under the Soviet occupation. Kim Il-sung came to consolidate his grip on the state power by eliminating or undermining rival political parties and their leaders including Jo Man-sik, Mu-jong, Park Heon-young, and Kim Du-bong (Oliver, 1993:188-189).

Between 1946 and 1948, the transitional government under the Soviet Occupation underwent a sweeping social and political change. In March 1946, it carried out a land reform, whereby land was freely distributed to farmers, while expropriating all assets of the Japanese residents and the properties of pro-Japan collaborators including big landowners without compensation. In June 1946, the transitional government nationalized all large-scale industries, mines, transportation and communication facilities,

---

[21] Kim Il-sung, born in 1912, was the leader of one of the Korean guerrilla groups against the Japanese.

and banks (Oliver, 1993:189). The interim government under Kim actively sponsored the expansion of mass educational programs as a crucial means to indoctrinate people with its own communist ideology. The number of schools in North Korea increased by tens and hundred times between 1945 and 1948. By 1948, North Korea managed to run 5000 middle schools, 69 technical schools, and 15 colleges. This is a stark contrast to the situation of Korea in 1945, when only 50 middle schools were existent in North Korea (Oliver, 1993:191).

South Korea under the US occupation (1945-1948)

Like the North, Koreans in the South wasted no time to set up grassroot organizations representing their interests and political goals. The most influential grass-root organization was the People's Committees that consisted of many civil groups and professional organizations including the Federation of Workers, the Peasants' Union, the Women's Federation, the League of Democratic Youth, and the Chondogyo religio-political organization (Oliver, 1993:187). About 145 People's Committees were already in operation, and, in fact, functioned like a form of self-government. While they were largely led by left-leaning Korean nationalists such as Lyeo Woon-hyung, the People's Committees enjoyed nation-wide support. Their popularity reflected the fact that Korean leftists and communists at that time were respected for their active role in the armed struggle against the Japanese. In addition, their call for a fair land reform attracted landless farmers, the majority of the Korean population at that time (Oliver, 1993:161).

On 6 September 1945, the People's Committees and other civic organizations proclaimed the Korean People's Republic. On the very same day, the American occupation forces landed at Incheon (a port city on South Korea's west coast) and established the American Military Government (AMG) in Seoul. The AMG considered the People's Committees as agents of the Soviet Union and therefore a threat to the US-centered order in Korea (Oliver, 1993:164). The AMG, thus, promptly ordered the people's committees and other Korean grassroot organizations such as the Federation of Workers to be disbanded (Oliver, 1993:162).

The local committees and labor unions, however, refused the AMG's order to be dissolved and openly advocated a fair land reform and a democratic constitution (Oliver, 1993:162). In December 1945, when the Moscow agreement on the trusteeship plan for Korea was announced, outraged Koreans took to the streets, carrying signs that read "Down with Trusteeship!" (Oliver, 1993:166). When Kim Gu (the leader of the Provisional Government of Korea) returned to South Korea in 1945, he formed the Korean Independence Party. He and his party opposed the 5 year-trusteeship. In some places in South Kyonsang and North Jeolla provinces, the local People's Committees organized protest rallies against the AMG. In response, the AMG imprisoned many leftists associated with the people's committees and this contributed to the growing Korean resentment toward the AMG (Oliver, 1993:174).

Instead of working with local grassroot organizations, the American military government (AMG) relied on pro-Japan collaborators (low level government officials under the Japanese rule), who were more amenable to the American geo-political interests, and on the affluent Koreans who could speak English.

Unlike the Russians who knew Korean independence fighters through their joint military campaigns against the Japanese, the Americans in the AMG did not even have a rudimentary understanding of Korean language and culture. Only a very few AMG advisors, mostly American missionaries, could speak Korean. Thus, they heavily relied on a small number of the Korean elite with English speaking ability (such as Rhee Seung-man) and their political friends who predominantly came from the affluent class and the milieu of the pro-Japan collaborators such as Kim Sung-soo. Together with the landowning elite, Kim Sung-soo, the owner of large textile mills and land at that time, established the Korean Democratic Party (KDP) as a political conduit to represent the interests of conservative Korean landowners who opposed the progressive land reform advocated by the People's Committees.

On 5 October 1945, the American Military Government established a Korean Advisory Committee and appointed Kim Song-soo as its chair. Eight of the total ten members of the Committee came from the conservative KDP (Oliver, 1993:164). Rhee Seung-man, who lived in the USA and spoke fluent English, aside from being an avid anti-Communist and pro-American, was chosen by the American Military Government to head the transitional government in the South.

Collaborating closely with the AMG, Rhee Seung-man launched an anti-communist campaign including radio shows. He argued in public that

"Communists were the enemies, rather than the supporters, of the Korean people" (Oliver, 1993:166). Rhee's anti-communist campaign was highly divisive since Koreans were largely sympathetic to leftist Korean independence groups. As the historian Oliver put it, there existed a "widespread appreciation of Communists, for the reason that the Soviet Union and the Communist Party had been their sole effective supporters during their long oppression by Japan" (Oliver, 1993:166). The pro-Japan collaborators including Korean police officers, who worked for the Japanese government, switched their side and now jumped on the bandwagon of anti-communist witch-hunts. In the name of "democracy" (only under American capitalism) and "freedom" (largely from Communism), they targeted Korean independence activists who fought against the Japanese. The post-liberation situation was perverse in the sense that the former henchmen for the Japanese imperialist government were now also the power-holders of "liberated" Korea and came to suppress the Korean independence fighters who made personal sacrifices for Korea's liberation. Conveniently, anti-communism became the justification for the continuing rule of the previous pro-Japan collaborators.

The political orientation of many Koreans in post-1945 Korea could be roughly categorized into three camps: the rightist, the leftist, and the moderate nationalist. Rhee Seung-man led the ultra right-wing camp that consisted of anti-communists, large landowners, and pro-Japanese collaborators. The leftist camp was made of people's Committees, the workers' party, the liberation army, and many idealistic university students. The moderate nationalist camp included the Korean Independence groups, led by Kim Gu, Kim Kyu-sic, Lyeo Woon-hyung, Jo Bong-am, John Myun Chang, among many others. Once in power, as in the case with Kim Il-sung, Rhee Seung-man began to undermine or eliminate his political rivals. For instance, Kim Gu and Ryeo Woon-hyung, the leading figures of the Korean Independence Movement, were eliminated by Rhee's supporters.

Korean Drama on the post-colonial Korea

The dramatization of the post-colonial period from 1945 and 1950 is highly controversial since it requires a critical inquiry into many historical events that are still debated. Indicative of the political challenges is the lack of TV series or films critical of the AMG. The series drama, "Land (땅)", for instance, was scheduled to air 50 episodes dealing with the Korean political situation after 1945. The Korea Broadcasting Service (KBS) had to stop airing the drama only after 15 episodes in 1991. The suspension of the TV drama was due to intense pressures from the conservative Korean establishment.

The situation has changed somewhat in the 2000s. The TV series, "Seoul 1945", for instance, sheds light on ideological conflicts in South Korea under the AMG government. As the drama portrays the main character as somewhat a progressive and leftist leaning intellectual, when it was aired, it drew heavy criticisms from right-wing civic groups intolerant to ideological diversity.

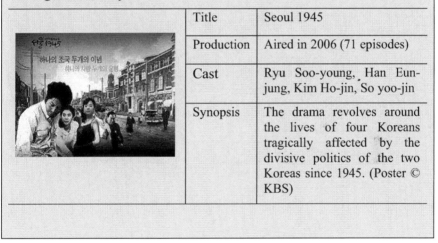

	Title	Seoul 1945
	Production	Aired in 2006 (71 episodes)
	Cast	Ryu Soo-young, Han Eun-jung, Kim Ho-jin, So yoo-jin
	Synopsis	The drama revolves around the lives of four Koreans tragically affected by the divisive politics of the two Koreas since 1945. (Poster © KBS)

In contrast to North Korea that swiftly carried out a popular land reform and other reform measures, the big landowners in South Korea with the backing of the AMG opposed any progressive land reform measure. Consequently, dissenters grew in numbers and anti-government protests sprang up in various places. The Busan-Daegu uprising of 1946, the April 3 Jeju uprising of 1948 and the Yeo-Soon mutiny were the major political incidents representative of the widespread opposition to the AMG and the transitional administration headed by Rhee Seung-man (Oliver, 1993:217).

Table 6.1 The chronology of major political events in South Korea, 1945 -1953

Year	Historical Events
August 1945	Japan's surrender and Korea's Liberation
September 1945	The proclamation of the Korean People's Republic (KPR) The American landing at Incheon The Establishment of the American Military Government The AMG disbands the People's Committees and the KPR.
December 1945	The Moscow Agreement for the 5-year trusteeship of Korea (administered by Russia, the US, Great Britain, and China).
September 1946	The Busan-Daegu Uprising
1947	Violating the Moscow agreement, the US proposed separate elections in the Koreas to be held in 1948, administered by the UN.
April 1948 -1949	The Jeju Uprising
May 1948	The creation of two separate states: the Republic of Korea (ROK) and the People's Democratic Republic of Korea (DPRK)
October 1948	The Yeosu-Suncheon Mutiny
1948 -1949	Leftist guerrilla insurgency in South Korea
1950-1953	The Korean War

The following is a brief summary of some popular protests in South Korea during the period between 1945 and 1949.

*The Busan-Daegu Uprising of 1946-47

In 1946, the railway workers in Busan, with the help of the South Korean Labor Party (남노당) and the People's Committees, went on a strike. A violent police crackdown on the striking workers led to more protests of strike supporters, spreading to Daegu, a neighboring city. The police killed more than 1000 civilians and arrested 25,000 people who were involved in the strike and the ensuing anti-government protests (Oliver 1993).

* The April 3rd Jeju Uprising

The main cause of the April 3rd Jeju Uprising was a widespread discontent among the Jeju residents toward the AMG. As in many cases of social protests, the trigger incident for the uprising was police brutality. In 1948, Jeju islanders gathered at a public demonstration to commemorate the March First Independence Movement of 1919. At the rally, a mounted police officer accidently injured a child with his horse but proceeded without caring for the injured. When the crowd of people that witnessed the incident began complaining, the police, instead of apologizing, used an excessive force to disperse the demonstration. In the process, six people were shot and killed. Outraged at the police brutality, 95% of Jeju residents went on a strike against the local authority but the government responded with mass arrests. From that moment onward, a series of violent clashes between outraged Jeju islanders and the local authority followed.

Amid the police crack-down on the Jeju people, the supporters of the People's Committee initiated an armed uprising against the Jeju local government on 3 April 1948. From the April Uprising, the conflict between the Jeju people and the AMG lasted for a year. By June 1948, over 6000 people were arrested. The local AMG responded with an extremely brutal manner by arresting and killing civilians including children. Hundreds and thousands of Jeju islanders went into mountains to escape the indiscriminate executions (Heo W, 2018). Following the order of Rhee Seung-man, the hunt for the people hiding in the mountains continued and resulted in the killing of hundreds and thousands of Jeju residents, including women and children, all in the name of anti-Communism.

The massacre in the aftermath of the April Jeju uprising, which was framed as a communist rebellion, was kept secret for almost six decades. According to a government report in 2003, about 20,000-30,000 people, which was about 10% of the population in Jeju at that time, fell victim to the armed conflict between 1948 and 1949. About 78.1 % of the victims were killed by the AMG forces, while the rest by the rebel forces (Heo W, 2018).

K-drama on the divisive politics during the post-colonial period

A few TV series and films shed light on the period of South Korea under the American occupation. They include: The Eyes of Dawn, The Taebaek Mountains, and Seoul 1945.

The TV series, "Eyes of Dawn" (also known as "Years of Upheaval), tells the story of three Koreans during the period from the Japanese occupation to the Korean War. Focusing on a love triangle between two men over one woman, the drama brought people's attention to the conflicts and sufferings of Koreans caught in Korea's ideological division.

	Title	The Eyes of Dawn (여명의 눈동자)
	Production	Aired 1991-1992 (36 episodes)
	Cast	Choi Jae-sung, Chae Shi-ra, Park Sang-won
	Synopsis	The drama tells a fictional story about a woman, who was forced to serve as a "comfort woman", and two men (Daechi and Harim) who loved her. One man was politically close to the communist North, while the other worked for the AMG.

Based on a novel by Kim Seong-Jong, this TV series was the first drama that openly dealt with highly controversial issues including the "comfort women" and the April 3rd Jeju Uprising. When it aired in 1992, it became a national hit with viewership rating reaching well over 50%.

Amid political suppression, a parliamentary election was held only in the South on 10 May 1948. The election was widely boycotted by major political parties and groups. Along with many organizations of Korean nationalists and leftists, Kim Gu's Korean Independence Party boycotted the 1948 election in the South. In the absence of major political rivals, Rhee Seungman and the Korean Democratic Party (KDP) of large landowners emerged as the main beneficiaries of the South only election (Pratt and Rutt 1999: 236). In July 1948, the National Assembly adopted the constitution of the Republic of Korea (ROK) and elected Rhee to President.

Meanwhile, parallel events took place in the North. The Supreme People's Assembly (572 members) in the North ratified the constitution for the Democratic People's Republic of Korea (DPRK) and elected Kim Il-sung as president (Oliver, 1993:207). The US-led United Nations (UN) approved the ROK as the only lawful government of Korea, while China and the Soviet Union recognized the DPRK as the only legitimate government (Oliver, 1993:208).

In South Korea, President Rhee Seungman carried out repressive measures which engendered more protests and rebellions, and even a partisan guerilla movement in the South. Notable examples were the Yeo-Soon Mutiny of 1948 and the leftist Partisan Struggle between 1948 and 1949.

* The Yeosu-Sooncheon Mutiny of 1948

In mid-October 1948, President Rhee ordered the Fourteenth Regiment in Yeosu (a southern port city), to crush the Jeju uprising. Refusing the order, the Korean soldiers organized a mutiny in Yeosu. The rebellion spread to Sooncheon, a neighboring city. Declaring martial law, President Rhee sent other troops to quell the mutiny. Eventually, the government force recaptured the two cities by the end of October. More than 2000 people were estimated to have been killed during the conflict between the rebel soldiers and the pro-government forces. In addition, close to 1000 people relating to the mutiny were convicted of treason and subsequently executed (Oliver, 1993:215-216).

* The Partisan Struggle of Korean Leftists, 1948-1949

Against this political backdrop, many Korean dissenters, led by the followers of the South Korean Labor Party, organized a guerrilla-style insurgency to overthrow the Rhee regime. After the failure of the Yeo-Soon mutiny, some two hundred rebel troops, escaped from Yeosu and Sooncheon, joined the guerrilla insurgency. Hiding in the large and deep Jiri mountain complex, they mounted armed attacks on the government forces (Oliver, 1993:216). Between 4th September 1948 and 30th April 1949, the Rhee regime arrested about 80,710 insurgents and dismissed about one third of the ROK army officers on the ground that they were sympathetic to the insurgents (Oliver, 1993:222). In December 1948, the government introduced the National Security Law (NSL) to purge all political dissenters who were suspected of being sympathetic to North Korea. The Rhee regime arrested some 90,000 people nationwide for the violation of the NSL (Pratt and Rutt 1999: 42).

	The Leftist Insurgency in the late 1940s	
	Based on Jo Jeong-rae's novel "Taebaegsanmaek", this film sheds light on the leftist guerrilla insurgency between 1948 and 1949. Focusing on their armed struggle in the Taebaek Mountains in the southern Jeolla province, the film provides an insight into the divisive ideological conflict that pitted Koreans against each other. Being critical to ideological extremism, the film depicts atrocities committed by both sides against innocent civilians.	
	Title	The Taebaek Mountains
	Released	1994
	Director	Im Kwon-taek
	Cast	Ahn Sung-ki, Kim Myung-gon, Kim Kap-soo, Shin Hyun-june, Oh Jung-hye
	Synopsis	The film follows the life of Kim Beom-woo, a Korean nationalist critical of ideological extremism.

The Korean War and the Inter-Korea Relations since 1953

With the establishment of two separate governments, the inter-Korea relationship further deteriorated. Between 1948 and 1950, the cross-border armed excursions and artillery attacks by both sides increased (Oliver 1993). The cross-border military conflicts further intensified after the withdrawal of the Soviet forces from the North in 1948 and the US forces from the South in 1949 (Pratt and Rutt 1999: 239). Meantime, the DPRK and ROK governments openly declared their intention to unify Korea by force, if necessary. The exchanges of war-mongering postures from both sides, accompanied by the increasing number of inter-Korea military conflicts at the border, eventually led to a full-blown civil war.

The Korean War (1950-1953)

On 25 June in 1950, the DPRK forces crossed the border to attack the ROK with the aim to reunify Korea under a communist regime. This Korean civil war soon developed into a regional war, as superpowers including the US, Russia, and China intervened in the war for their own geopolitical interests.

When North Korea controlled almost all territory of South Korea, except its southern coastal areas, the US intervened in the Korean civil war to restore the Rhee regime. With the intervention of the US, the tide of the war turned against North Korea, as the USA brought in American and Allied forces under the auspices of the UN. When the American forces took control of almost all Korea except only the far northern area close to China, Beijing decided to intervene in the Korean War to prevent the establishment of an anti-Chinese government right at its border. Beijing sent 2.97 million Chinese soldiers to support Pyongyang, while the Soviets provided North Korea with aircover and technological support (China Daily, June 28, 2010). The two sides were engaged in fierce battles causing millions of casualties until the war came to a stalemate. Eventually, North Korea, China and the USA came to agree on a cease-fire.

President Rhee Seung-man of South Korea, however, refused to sign the armistice agreement, calling for the prolongation of the war with the goal of unifying the entire country in the South's favor (KOCIS 2019). To ensure that the South would not violate the truce agreement, the USA forced Rhee to accept restrictions on Korean sovereignty by keeping Korean troops under US command. In return, the US promised to guarantee the ROK's security by leaving American troops in the country to protect South Korea from potential North Korean attacks (Oliver, 1993:247). Even as of this writing, the South Korean military is still under the control of the American government. It should be noted that the Moon Jae-in administration is currently seeking to regain Korea's military commandship from the USA.

The devasting Korean War left millions of casualties and enormous destruction of properties and cultural heritage. About 3 million Koreans and some 33,600 American soldiers lost their lives (Oliver, 1993:225 and 236), while close to 180,000 Chinese soldiers perished during the war (China Daily June 28, 2010).

The Korean War, however, greatly benefited Japan both diplomatically and economically. Since Japan was logistically the best place for American troops in Asia during the Korean War, Washington purchased its war-related supplies and its Korea-aid materials from Japan. With the help of Washington purchasing two-thirds of Japan's total exports between 1951 and 1953, the Korean War played a crucial role in reviving Japan's war-torn economy (Oliver, 1993:245). Without the Korean War and the American support, Japan would not have been able to recover so quickly its devastated economy. Moreover, the Korean War helped Japan to forge a close political tie with the USA relatively soon after WWII.

Films on the Korean War (1950-1953)

Most South Korean films on the Korean War tend to portray North Koreans as evil villains by blaming them for starting the civil war. They also tend to present the USA as a hero, fighting for Korea's freedom and democracy. Conservative political groups and parties in South Korea often sponsor the production of films focusing on the American intervention in 1950 and the subsequent battle of Incheon that became a turning point for the Korean War in favor of the ROK. Released in 1981, the film, "Incheon", for instance, depicts the Korean War with the focus on the American General MacArthur. The film was financed by Moon Sun-myeong's Unification Church, an anti-communist Christian cult group.

Another Korean War film, "Operation of Incheon: Operation Chromite" (2016), focuses on the role of a Korean intelligence unit in gathering information on the North Korean military before the American landing operation at Incheon. While conservative Koreans tend to worship General MacArthur as a national hero, others take a critical approach to his role in the Korean War. They argue that MacArthur was responsible for several massacres of innocent civilians during the Korean War.

In contrast to the pro-American films on the Korean War, several films such as "Tae Geuk Gi", stand out for their humanist approach, emphasizing the sameness of Korean nation, while critiquing ideological extremism of the both sides.

The film, "Tae Geuk Gi: The Brotherhood of War", tells a fictional story about two brothers who were forced to fight in the Korean War on the opposite sides. Rather than portraying the Korean War as a glorious war against "the evil communist North Korea", the film depicts the war as a senseless civil war that pit family members and neighbors against each other.

	Title	Tae Geuk Gi: The Brotherhood of War
	Released	2004
	Director	Kang Je-gyu
	Cast	Jang Dong-gun, Won Bin, Lee Eun-ju, Jo Yoon-hee, Gong Hyung-jin,
	Synopsis	The ideological polarization pit family members, lovers, and neighbors against each other. Focusing on the older brother's love toward his younger sibling, it depicts innocent Korean civilians who fell victim to the Korean War. (poster © Showbox/Mediaplex)

Together with "Tae Geuk Gi", the film, "The Front Line", also sheds a critical light on the Korean War.

	Title	The Front Line (고지전)
	Released	2011
	Director	Jang Hoon
	Cast	Shin Ha-kyung and Go Soo
	Synopsis	While negotiations for a cease-fire are underway, the two sides fiercely fight over the area that would become the future dividing line between North Korea and South Korea. (poster ©Showbox/ TPS company)

Inter-Korea Relations since 1953

Since the USA and North Korea never signed a peace treaty, the two Koreas are technically still at war. What is perverse is the fact that South Korea, even if it wishes, cannot sign a peace treaty without the consent of the USA, since it is not one of the signatories to the 1953 ceasefire agreement. In the absence of a peace treaty, continuing military tensions resulting from large-scale military exercises and an arms race continue to undermine democracy and peaceful economic developments in the Koreas. In both countries, security concerns have been used as a political justification for the curtailment of civil rights and the suppression of dissents. Cultural and economic exchanges and communication between the North and the South have been outright banned for most times. (Park, M 2018). Hostility between the two Koreas manifested itself in numerous forms including bombing and assassination attempts against the leaders of the both sides in the 1960s and 1970s.

Films on Inter-Korea Hostility

The film "Silmido" is based on a true story of a South Korean secret military unit whose mission was to infiltrate North Korea to assassinate Kim Il-sung, the leader of the DPRK (Oliver, 1993:299).

	Title	Silmido (실미도)
	Production	Released in 2003 (Directed by Kang Woo-suk)
	Cast	Sol Kyung-gu, Ahn Sung-ki, Jeong Jae-young, Im Won-hee, Heo Jun-ho
	Synopsis	With the mission to assassinate Kim Il-Sung, the South Korean secret squad undergoes intensive, inhuman training on Silmido, off the coast of Incheon. Suddenly dropping the project, the authority tries to silence the squad. (poster © Cinema Service)

Between 1968 and 1971, the South Korean special military squad underwent extremely gruelling training which resulted in 7 deaths among

---

150

the 31 recruits. In 1972, Nixon's visit to China led to a rapprochement between the USA and China. Fearing about the abandonment by their political sponsors (China and the USA), the North and the South became concerned about their own security and survival. In this context, the South Korean President Park initiated a joint-talk with the North Korean regime in 1972 (Oliver, 1993:301). When the two Koreas began formal discussions, the secret assassination project was dropped by the Park regime. Meantime, the members of the secret squad who endured an extremely inhumane training, did not receive proper compensation nor any recognition of their work for the government. As they rebelled, the truth about the secret project came to light.

As in the case with the film, "Silmido", the TV series drama, "City Hunter", deals with the same secret mission to infiltrate North Korea. Using the historical event as a background for a revenge plot, it mainly focuses on a romance story, spiced up with scenes of action and counter-intelligence operation.

Title	City Hunter
Aired	2011 (20 episodes)
Cast	Lee Min-ho, Park Min-yeong
Synopsis	The South Korean military eliminates the special squad that took part in the secret mission to assassinate North Korean leaders. A lone survivor is determined to avenge for the fallen squad members. He and his adopted son, after a long period of training and preparation, return to Korea on a revenge mission. (poster © sbs)

The inter-Korea relations greatly improved by the late 1990s. Especially, the South Korean administrations led by President Kim Dae-Jung (1998-2003) and President Roh Moo-hyun (2003-2008) of South Korea, made significant efforts (known as the "Sunshine policy") to ease military tensions on the Korean peninsula (Park, M 2018). Starting from 1998, the two Koreas carried out joint projects to foster economic cooperation and cultural exchange. As part of the inter-Korea partnership, South Korea's Hyundai built tourist resorts in North Korea's Geumgang mountain region and the governments of the two Koreas agreed on the construction of oil pipelines across the Korean peninsula (Pratt and Rutt 1999: 99). In June 2000, a historic inter-Korea summit was held for the first time in Pyongyang as the leaders of the two Koreas met to discuss inter-Korea cooperation.

Korea as One

The film, "Korea as One", takes a humanist approach, emphasizing the sameness of Korean nation. It depicts the historical events surrounding the first Unified Korea Sports team since the Korean War. In the 1991 World Table Tennis Championship in Japan, the Unified Korean team won the gold medal.

	Title	Korea as One
	Production	Released in 2012 (Directed by Moon Hyeon-sung)
	Cast	Ha Ji-won, Bae Doo-na
	Synopsis	The best table tennis players of the two Koreas formed a united group to compete at the 41st World Table Tennis Championship. The film follows the development of friendship among the united team members. It depicts how they overcome mutual suspicion, hostility, and rivalry to forge a genuine friendship. (poster © CJ Entertainment)

The diplomatic efforts towards peaceful-coexistence, consistent throughout the period of the Kim and Roh administrations between 1998 and 2008, did not sit well with the American government's policy on North Korea. The US administration led by George W. Bush designated North Korea as an "axis of evil" along with Iran and Iraq, and consequently made North Korea fearful of its survival. With the US-North Korea relations hit an all-time low,

Pyongyang accelerated its drive to nuclear armament. The troubled relations between Washington and Pyongyang subsequently increased military tensions and seriously undermined South Korea's "Sunshine" policy to foster a peaceful co-existence and cooperation on the Korean Peninsula (Park, M 2018).

Films on Inter-Korea Détente in the 1990s

With the historical backdrop of the North-South political détente period in the 1990s, the film, "Shiri", is a fictional story about North Korea's military hardliners who try to provoke a war with the South.

	Title	Shiri
	Released	1999
	Producer	Byeon Moo-rim, Lee Kwan-hak
	Cast	Han Suk-kyu, Choi Min-shik, Kim Yoon-jin, and Song Kang-ho
	Synopsis	Set in the time period of 1990s, a team of North Korean commandoes has the plan to start a war. The film tells a fictional story about the plan gets foiled by South Korea's special agents (poster © IDP studio)

In the late 2000s, the inter-Korea relations began to deteriorate under South Korea' conservative administrations led by Lee Myung-bak and Park Geun-hye. They dropped the Sunshine policy of their predecessors and instead pursued a hardline policy on North Korea. The Park administration even shut down the Gaesung-industrial complex, the symbol of inter-Korean economic cooperation.

Starting from 2017, the South Korean administration under Moon Jae-in has restarted the peaceful diplomatic approach to ease tension on the Korean peninsula by holding two inter-Korean summits. The geo-political dynamics surrounding the Korean peninsular is, however, seemingly unfavorable to the peaceful co-existence and development of the two Koreas. It is argued that Washington, seeking to contain the rising China and Russia in East Asia, would unlikely lift economic sanctions on North Korea and normalize its relations with Pyongyang by signing a peace treaty.

North Korea and the American military- industrial complex

The film "King 2 Heart" stands out for its take on Korean unification. What is notable about this drama is that it emphasizes Korean nationalism regardless of ideological differences, while presenting the American military- industrial complex as an obstacle to Korea's unification.

	Ttitle	The King 2 Hearts
	Production	Aired 2012 (20 episodes)
	Cast	Ha Ji-won, Lee Sung-gi
	Synopsis	In a fictional South Korea having a constitutional monarchy, the crown prince falls for a North Korean woman, a daughter of an influential government official in North Korea. Their love is put to the test by divergent oppositional forces. Is their love strong enough to overcome all challenges and obstacles? (poster © MBC)

The tragedy of the divided Korea lies in the fact that Korea occupies a strategic place in geopolitical rivalry between the US-led world order and its challengers (Russia and China). In this geo-political context, a peaceful co-existence of two Koreas cannot be solely determined by Koreans themselves. Any approach to inter-Korean relations should be reckoned with the consideration of clashing geopolitical interests of Korea's neighbors in the Asia-Pacific region.

K-Drama and Films on North Korea

Except some films sponsored by conservative governments and right-wing civic groups, most films and dramas on the post-war inter-Korean relationship tend to fall into one of three categories. The first is the one that takes a humanist approach critical to ideological extremism. Films such as "Joint Security Area" and "Korea as One" belong to this category. The second category is the one that focuses on Hollywood style escapism. Most films in this category tend to be action-packed thrillers. For instance, blockbuster films like "The Berlin File", "Steel Rain", and "Confidential Assignment" all focus on fighting scenes involving secret North Korean agents with superb martial arts skills. The third category is the one that emphasizes the sameness of the Korean nation, while presenting some internal and external forces that get in the way of inter-Korean reconciliation. The TV series, "King 2 Hearts", belongs to the third category. In general, neither TV series, movies nor documentary films depict North Korea and inter-Korea relations from a balanced perspective, largely due to political censorship. The appendix at the end of this book contains a selected list of TV series and films about the division of Korea and the post-war inter-Korea relations.

Contemporary Films on Inter-Korea Relations

In sharp contrast to most films on North Korea, the film, "Joint security area JSA", tells a fictional story about a secret friendship between North and South Korean soldiers at the JSA in the DMZ. The movie is heartwarming and tragic at the same time.

Title	Joint Security Area JSA
Production	2000
Director	Park Chan-wook
Cast	Lee Young-ae, Song Kang-ho, Lee Byung-hun, Shin Ha-kyun
Synopsis	A fatal shooting takes place in the DMZ (Demilitarized Zone) that divides the Koreas. An UN-led investigation into the shooting reveals a secret friendship between the North Korean and South Korean soldiers. (poster © CJ entertainment)

The film "The Berlin File" is a Hollywood style action movie. It tells a fictional story about North Korean staff members in the DPRK embassy in Berlin.

Title	The Berlin File
Released	2013
Director	Ryu Seung-wan
Cast	Ha Jung-woo, Han Suk-gyu, Jun Ji-hyun, and Ryu Seung-beom
Synopsis	A North Korean agent finds himself in a conspiracy involving high-rank officials of the North Korean army. As he and his wife are set up as a scapegoat, they find themselves on the run. With the help of a South Korean agent, they uncover the truth behind the Berlin file. (poster © CJ Entertainment)

The blockbusters action movie, "Confidential Assignment", tells the fictional story about an inter-Korea operation to capture North Korean criminals who escaped to South Korea. As in the case with the Berlin File, the film perpetuates negative stereotypes of North Koreans, supposedly engaging in illegal drug smuggling or money counterfeiting.

	Title	Confidential Assignment
	Released	2017
	Director	Kim Sung-hoon
	Cast	Hyun Bin, Yoo Hae-jin
	Synopsis	A North Korean counterfeit money making operation goes awry when a insider steals the master plate and runs away to South Korea. A North Korean officer from the special investigation unit is sent to South Korea to find the thief. His investigation in South Korea is possible under one condition. He must work with a South Korean detective. (poster © CJ Entertainment)

Chapter 7

From Dictatorship to Democracy: The Contemporary Politics of South Korea

This chapter outlines major political events in South Korea since the establishment of the Republic of Korea (ROK) in 1948. Focusing on the reasons for regime change, it provides a historical context of major political upheavals and social movements under all administrations of the ROK, listed in table 7.1. The historical overview is accompanied by information on relevant TV series dramas and films.

Table 7.1 Chronology of the South Korean Administrations, 1948-2019

Rhee Seungman (1948-1960), Park Chung-hee (1960-1979), Roh Tae-woo (1988-1993), Kim Yong-sam (1993-1998), Kim Dae-jung (1998-2002), Roh Moo-hyeon (2003-2008), Lee Myeong-bak (2009-2012), Park Geun-hye (2012-2016), Moon Jae-in (2017- 2022)

The Rhee Seung-man Administration (1948-1960)

The 1948 National Assembly election, resulting in the establishment of the Republic of Korea (ROK), was deeply flawed since it was held amid widespread election boycotts and the suppression of left-leaning political activism. The elected members of the National Assembly, mostly from the Democratic Party of conservative landowners, appointed Rhee Seung-man to the position of President.

President Rhee was an avid anti-communist with strong autocratic dispositions. As in the case with North Korea, challengers to the power-holders did not fare well. Rhee's rivals soon vanished from the national political scenes. In 1949, Kim Gu (the premier of the Provisional

Government in Shanghai) was assassinated by Ahn Doo-hee, a military officer. Given the fact that Ahn only served on year in jail and was later promoted to a colonel, he was believed to have followed orders from President Rhee and his supporters (Tudor 2012:86).

With a series of anti-democratic measures, Rhee firmly entrenched his autocratic rule in South Korea. The Rhee administration enacted the draconian National Security Law (NSL) which defined anti-state activity so broadly that it empowered the state to punish anyone who is critical to the status quo. Once charged with the violation of the NSL, the violator could be punished by death or life-sentence (Oliver, 1993: Cumings, 2002). Within less than one year after the introduction of NSL, about 30,000 people were charged with the violation of the National Security Law (Tudor 2012:85).

In 1951, Rhee established the Liberal Party, a conservative party loyal to President Rhee, to counter the increasingly assertive Democratic Party that sought to reduce presidential power. Throughout the 1950s, the Rhee administration used various means, from vote buying to political coercion and threats, to have the predominantly rural populace of South Korea elect Rhee and his Liberal Party to power (Tudor 2012:86). In 1954, Rhee forced the National Assembly to remove the limit on the number of terms a president could serve, allowing him to be president for life (Tudor 2012:85).

* The April Student Revolution

Mass protests against Rhee's dictatorship erupted in 1960. Known as the April 19th Student Revolution (sa-il-goo hyukmyeong), the nationwide protest against Rhee's autocratic rule, was largely led by high school and university students. For the Presidential election of 1960, the regime seized ballot boxes to manipulate the votes in favor of Rhee's re-election (Oliver, 1993:262). The triggering incident of the April Student Revolution was the revelation of the vote rigging and the death of a student protestor at one of the ensuing street demonstrations denouncing the election fraud. Initially led by middle-and-high school students[22], the first peaceful protest was held on

---

[22] By 1956 more than 91 percent of all children aged 6-11 were enrolled in elementary schools (Oliver, 1993:259). By 1960 South Korea had 73 degree-granting colleges with an enrollment of 80,000 students. This meant that South Korea had more college students per capita than England in 1960 (Cumings, 2002: 25).

March 15 in the southern city of Masan. When a middle-school student was killed by a tear gas canister, the police tried to cover up his death by throwing his body into the sea. The truth soon surfaced when his body, with a debris of the tear gas canister still stuck in his eye socket, floated up to the shore. Outraged at the police brutality and its cover-up, citizens joined a series of anti-government protest that quickly spread to other cities including the capital, Seoul.

On 18 April 1960, about 3000 students in Seoul took to the streets (Oliver, 1993:263). On the next day, the number of protestors swelled to about 100,000 and they peacefully marched to the Blue House to present a petition to President Rhee. Similar protests were held in other cities including Masan, Gwangju, and Daejeon. Rhee's response was brutal. The soldiers opened fire into the protestors, killing 200 and injuring more than six thousands (Pratt and Rutt 1999: 15; Tudor 2012:86; Oliver, 1993:263). After the death of hundreds of students, civil disobedience spread like a wildfire. University professors came forward to the frontline of the protest, calling for Rhee's resignation (Pratt and Rutt 1999: 15; Tudor 2012:86). Even the police and the military decided to disobey the orders to shoot. On 26th April, due to pressure from the military as well as the US government that was increasingly concerned about the political instability of South Korea, President Rhee resigned and fled to Hawaii, under American protection (Oliver, 1993:263; Tudor 2012:86; Pratt and Rutt 1999: 15).

After Lee's departure, South Korea experienced a political spring whereby political parties were revived and media outlets proliferated. Jo Bong-am's Progressive Party re-emerged as the Popular Socialist Party, while Kim Ku's Independence Party was also revived. Newspapers and periodicals increased from around 600 to nearly 1,600 with some 160,000 reporters (Oliver, 1993:267). During this time, South Korea had more newspaper readers per capita than almost any country in the world (Cumings, 2002: 25).

The April Student Revolution of 1960

Several films deal with Korean politics under the Rhee Seung-man regime. The TV series, "The First Republic", sheds light on the domestic politics under the Rhee Seung-man administration, while the TV drama, "My Sister's March", deals with students' protests against the election fraud, which paved the way to the April Student Revolution in 1960.

	Title	My Sister's March
	Production	Aired in 2010 (2 episodes)
	Cast	Jung Chan, Kim Gyeong-rae
	Synopsis	The drama tells a story about participants in the Masan protest in March 15, 1960, that sparked the April student protests. (poster © mbc)

University students were vocal about the future policy direction of the ROK. Critiquing the government's lenient attitude toward corrupt politicians who served for the previous Rhee regime, students demanded harsher punishments for the wrong-doers. They even touched the extremely sensitive issue, Korean reunification, that was previously a forbidden topic for open discussion. Students demanded that they hold meetings with the North Korean counterpart to discuss the prospect of peaceful reunification with the North (Oliver, 1993:267). "Seoul's Spring", however, ended abruptly, as the Korean military stepped into the political scenes through a military coup in May 1961.

The film, "The President's Barber", depicts the political situation surrounding the fall of the Rhee regime to the rise of the Park Chung-hee regime.

	Title	The President's Barber (효자동 이발사)
	Released	2004
	Director	Im Chan-sang
	Cast	Song Gang-ho, Moon So-ri
	Synopsis	Through the eyes of a barber and his family, the film depicts Korea's turbulent politics in the 1960s. It takes a satirical approach to the politics of anti-communism under the administration of Park Chung-hee. (poster © showbox)

The Park Chung-Hee Administration (1961-1979)

After seizing power through a coup d'état in May 1961, General Park Chung stayed in power for the next 18 years. The rise of Park to power was indicative of the status of pro-Japanese collaborators in the South after Korea's liberation from Japan in 1945. Pro-Japan collaborators, by and large, escaped a punishment, because the American military government in the South heavily relied on the moneyed class and former-police officers to govern the highly volatile populace. Park Chung-hee was one of the pro-Japan collaborators. During the colonial era, Park served as a high-rank military officer for the Japanese army. In 1937, he enrolled in Japan's Manchurian Military Institute, from which he was admitted to the prestigious Tokyo Imperial Military Institute. While serving in the Manchuria-based Kwantung Army, he rose to the position of first lieutenant (Oliver, 1993:278). According to the Institute for Research on Collaborationist Activists, Park made a pledge of allegiance in 1939 to Imperial Japan and its army, written in blood, "I am both physically and spiritually ready to be a Japanese subject and am willing to give my life for the emperor" (The Korea Times, 8 November 2009).

For both internal and external reasons, Park Chung-hee normalized the diplomatic relations with Japan, despite the strong opposition from the Korean people. First of all, the US government pressured South Korea to normalize its diplomatic relations with Japan, as Washington saw the ROK-Japan cooperation as a crucial pillar to its geopolitical strategy to contain the communist bloc in Asia.

An equally important factor for the normalization was the lobby of Japanese businesses. According to a report by the CIA (Central Intelligence Agency), between 1961 and 1965, six Japanese corporations provided illegal political funds of USD 66,000,000 to Park's political party, the Democratic Republican Party (Minju-gonghwa-dang 민주공화당). During the same period, two thirds of the revenue for Park's party came from the Japanese corporations (Kim, et.al. 2018). Another contributing factor was Korea's dependence on foreign capital to revive its economy through a rapid industrialization. One of the main foreign credit lenders included Japan.

Park Chung-hee's Normalization Treaty with Japan faced a strong domestic opposition, due to Japan's unapologetic attitude toward its colonial past. Japan has been denying its responsibility for the forced Korean labor and sexual slavery of Korean women. Meantime, Japan has glorified its colonial rule over Korea, while it claims that Korea benefited from Japan's rule because Japan "modernized" Korea by building railways and factories (of course, not mentioning the real reason, for Japan's own economic and military benefits). In 1951, Japan stated that it would not accept Korean demand for "reparations" and instead demanded repayment for the industrial and transport facilities that Japan had built in Korea (Oliver, 1993:294). Japan's arrogant and unapologetic attitude was equally reflected in its disparaging and discriminatory measures toward Korean residents in Japan[23] (Oliver, 1993:292).

---

[23] About 800,000 ethnic Koreans in Japan were denied of citizenship and suffered various forms of discrimination. Until 1990, all Koreans in Japan were finger-printed by the police (Oliver, 1993:292).

Despite strong domestic opposition, the Park government signed the Normalization Treaty with Japan in 1965. According to the Korea-Japan Treaty, Japan agreed to pay US$300 million "as a gesture of goodwill but emphatically not as reparation" to South Korea and it would also lend $500 million as an economic loan to the Park administration. In return, Park agreed that South Korea would not make any future compensation claims regarding the Japanese occupation of Korea (Pratt and Rutt 1999: 231).

The Treaty provoked widespread opposition from the populace who were outraged at the terms of normalization and more importantly, the absence of Japan's apology. As Park hastily concluded a normalization treaty with Japan, without the consent of Korean victims themselves, the Korean public was outraged that the Park regime sold out Koreans for just $300 million and outright abandoned the Korean government's right to demand a fair compensation for the Korean victims. Large segments of the population led by university students and opposition parties organized public demonstrations denouncing the treaty (Oliver, 1993:293). Hundreds of students went on hunger strikes, while others took part in class boycotts. Many professors signed petitions to demand the government and all political parties to reject the shamefully unequal treaty with Japan. As students took to the streets demanding the nullification of the treaty, the Park government put the country under martial laws and sent troops into the university campuses to quell the protests (Pratt and Rutt 1999: 231).

The legacy of Park's rule is contentious. On one hand, he has been praised for South Korea's rapid economic development. On the other hand, he has been criticized for the gross violation of human rights under his dictatorial rule. As for his economic legacy, the Park administration carried out a state-led industrialization project and an export-oriented economic policy throughout the 1960s and 1970s. To this end, the Park administration required a large sum of capital and technology as well as international markets for Korean exports. Park Chung-hee turned to the USA and Japan as its close economic partners. The USA opened its markets to South Korea and purchased Korean products especially for the American troops during the Vietnam War. In return, the Park administration made the "trade-off" agreement with the US, whereby the ROK sent its troops to support the Americans in the Vietnam War (Oliver, 1993:295).

Meantime, the Park administration promoted the export of Korean labor (as miners, nurses, and construction workers), as it needed foreign currencies in the form of workers' remittances. For instance, the Park regime made an agreement with the German counterpart that South Korea would send thousands of workers to German coal mines in exchange for Germany's financial aid of 150 million Deutsche Marks. Starting from 1963, South Korea sent almost 8,000 workers to coal mines in Germany and the "miner-for-aid swap" continued until 1977 (Korea Times, 24 February 2010).

The South Korean Workers in the 1960s and 70s

The film, "Ode to My Father (국제시장)", sheds light on the contribution of ordinary Korean workers to South Korea's rapid economic development throughout the 1960s and 1970s.

	Title	Ode to My Father (국제시장)
	Released	2014
	Director	Yoon Je-kyoon and Park Ji-seong
	Cast	Hwang Jung-min, Kim Yun-jin
	Synopsis	The film follows the life story of Deok-soo who runs an importing store in Gookje Market. From the period of the Korea War to the present-day South Korea, the movie shows the lives of ordinary Korean workers who made personal sacrifices to support their families and thereby contributed to Korea's economic development. (Poster © CJ entertainment)

By and large, the film, "Ode to My Father", depicts the life of ordinary Korean workers including the Korean miners and nurses sent to Germany. The film focuses on the personal sacrifices of Korean workers to support their loved ones. Lacking a critical approach to the Vietnam War, the film, however, portrays Korean soldiers as caring people, rather than foreign mercenaries who fought for the American geopolitical interests in Vietnam.

On a closer examination, South Korea's impressive economic growth in the 1970s and 1980s was possible mainly due to hard-working Korean workers. Park's own contribution to South Korea's economic development has been greatly exaggerated. Furthermore, Park's economic policy disproportionally benefited large conglomerates (Chaebeol) and Park's main political supporters in Taegu-Kyuongsang provinces. Fostering a close relationship with large corporations, the Park regime allowed big businesses to exploit workers by banning all forms of industrial action and freedom of speech.

Throughout the 1970s, Park issued a series of extremely repressive decrees to muzzle opposition. He set up a Central Intelligence Agency to root out dissenters. In 1971, a Special Law for National Protection was passed to curtail citizen's rights of mobility, public assembly and freedom of speech and press. Park promulgated a new "Yushin (revitalization)" constitution that abolished the direct presidential election and the limit on the presidential term. The Yushin constitution also curtailed the power of the National Assembly, as one thirds of its members had to be presidential appointees and its annual meetings were reduced to only 2 weeks (Oliver, 1993:304).

Jeon Tae-il

The film, "A Single Spark (아름다운 청년 전태일)", is based on the true story of Jeon Tae-il, a garment factory worker in Seoul.

	Title	A Single Spark
	Released	1995
	Director	Park Gwang-soo
	Cast	Moon Sung-geun, Hong Gyeong-in
	Synopsis	The film tells the life story of Jeon Tae-il through the eyes of a student activist, Kim Yong-su. As Kim learns about Jeon's death, he meets Jeon's co-workers and discovers the exploitive sweatshop working conditions. (Poster © Age of Planning)

On 13 November in 1970, Jeon Tae-il, set fire to himself to bring public attention to the sweatshop working condition and the lack of workers' rights in South Korea. Before his death, he shouted "Abide by Basic Law concerning Workers! We are not machines!" His self-immolation served as a spark for labor activism that culminated in massive industrial actions and the establishment of trade unions in the late 1980s.

The government replaced autonomous student representative bodies with a state-organized militaristic student organization (Lee N 2002). University campuses were under surveillance of plain-clothed police officers, while dissenters faced imprisonment, torture, or dismissal from school or workplace. As hundreds and thousands of political dissidents were imprisoned throughout the 1960s and 1970s, the pro-democracy movement went underground.

Political Suppression in the 1970s

The film, "The Aesthetics of Yushin" (유신의 미학), sheds light on the pro-democracy student movement in the 1970s.

	Title	The Aesthetics of Yushin
	Released	2014
	Director	Kim No-gyeong
	Cast	Kim Dong-hyeon, Kim Hyeo-bi
	Synopsis	The film tells a fictional story about a university student who was involved in the Association of Democratic Student Youths (Mincheonghakryeon), an illegal student organization in 1974. (Poster © Kim No-gyeong)

In 1974, the Park Chung-hee regime framed the Association of Democratic Student Youths (ADSU: Mincheonghakryeon) as a communist organization, and imprisoned hundreds of students, who were allegedly involved in the ADSU, with the charge of the violation of National Security Law.

Despite police surveillance, many brave students organized clandestine circles of activists and held flash street demonstrations (Lee N 2002). In 1979, hundreds of university students in Busan and Masan organized demonstrations (known as the Buma Uprising) calling for the abolishment of military dictatorship. The pro-democracy protests began to spread to other parts of the country. Against this backdrop of civil unrest, Park Chung-hee was assassinated by Kim Jae-gyu, the director of the Korean Central Intelligence Agency, who had deep political disagreements with Park Chung-hee (Park, M 2018).

TV series dramas on the Park Chung-hee administration

The TV series, "The Third Republic", shed light on Korean politics under the Park regime in the 1960s.

Title	The Third Republic
Aired	1993 (26 Episodes)
Cast	Lee Soon-jae
Synopsis	The drama depicts the military coup of 1961 and the political processes leading to the establishment of the 1972 "Yushin (Revitalization)" constitution that seriously undermined civil rights. (Poster ©MBC)

The TV series drama, "The Fourth Republic", sheds light on the major political events between 1972 and 1979 under the rule of Park Chung-hee.

Title	The Fourth Republic
Aired	1995-1996 (MBC)
Cast	Lee Chang-hwan, Park Geun-hyeong,
Synopsis	The drama is a sequel to the MBC's "The Third Republic". It deals with the political situation between 1972 and 1979, leading to the Buma Uprising and the assassination of Park. (Poster ©MBC)

The Chun Doo-hwan Administration (1980-1987)

With Park Chung-hee removed, civil society enjoyed a brief period of political spring, whereby civic activism for democratization was expressed in the form of political gatherings, protests, and critical press. However, the military junta frustrated people's aspiration for democracy once again, as General Chun Doo-Hwan seized power through a coup d'état in December 1979.

The coup was met with nation-wide, massive student demonstrations opposing the rule of the military. Some 100,000 students from 30 universities took part in the demonstration on 15 May 1980. In response, Chun Doo-hwan put the entire country under a martial law which prohibited all political activities (Oliver, 1993:315). Leaders of the main opposition party such as Kim Dae-jung were arrested and imprisoned.

* The Gwangju Massacre of 1980

As in the case with Seoul, massive student demonstrations were held in Gwangju, a southern city in Jeolla province, against the military coup. General Chun despatched Special Warfare Commandos (the toughest military force in South Korea) to crack down on the pro-democracy movement. Between 18 May and 27 May, the special troopers indiscriminately killed over hundreds of citizens (Cumings, 2002:26).

K-drama and films on the Gwangju Massacre of 1980

Since the mid 1990s, several films have been produced to shed critical light on the military dictatorship under the Chun Doo-hwan regime. The historical events involving the Gwangju massacre was explored in several films and TV series. They include: "Splendid Holiday" and "Taxi Driver", "Sandglass", "The Fifth Republic", "A Taxi Driver", "Ordinary People", "The Old Garden", and "26 Years".

The film, "A Petal" (released in 1996), depicts the Gwangju Uprising. The film was censored by the governmental body for performing arts when it was released in 1996. It was ordered to remove the slogan, that appeared

---

on the film advertisement, which states "Punish the murderer, Chun Doo-hwan!"

	Title	A Petal (꽃잎)
	Released	1996 (Director: Jang Sun-woo)
	Cast	Lee Jung Hyun, Moon Sung-keun
	Synopsis	The film focuses on a girl who witnessed the murder of her mother by the Korean Special troops in Gwangju in 1980. (poster © Miracin Korea)

The film, "Taxi Driver", is based on the real story of a taxi driver who helped German reporter Jürgen Hinzpeter to enter Gwangju city, amid the media blockage of the Chun regime's suppression of the Gwangju uprising. Hinzpeter managed to film the Gwangju massacre and exposed his video footage to the world. Drawing on Hinzpeter's video footage, several documentary films on the massacre became circulated in underground student circles throughout the 1980s. Those documentary films greatly facilitated political activism of university students against the military dictatorship under Chun Doo-hwan.

	Title	A Taxi Driver
	Released	2017 (Director: Jang Hoon)
	cast	Song Kang-ho, Thomas Kretschmann
	Synopsis	The film tells a true story about a German reporter and a Taxi driver. As the reporter films the unfolding events, he becomes the target of Chun's special military squad. The taxi driver, who smuggled the German reporter to Gwangju, helps the journalist to escape, so that the truth about the Gwangju massacre could come to light. (poster © Showbox/ The Lamp)

In contrast to most Gwangju-related films focusing on victims' perspective, the film, "Peppermint Candy (박하사탕)," tells the story of a man who worked for the oppressive Chun regime. It depicts the traumas and the guilt of a soldier who had to kill the protestors in Gwangju.

Different from the historical films mentioned above, "26 Years" is a historical fusion movie, based on a webcomic. It follows a story about a group of five Koreans who try to assassinate the man responsible for the Gwangju massacre.

The film, "Splendid Holiday (화려한 휴가 aka May 18)", depicts political events leading up to the Gwangju massacre of 1980. The film title is the actual code name of the mission given to the special forces to crack down on the protestors in Gwangju.

	Title	Splendid Holiday
	Released	2007 (Director: Kim Ji-hoon)
	Cast	Kim Sang-kyung, Ahn Sung-ki
	Synopsis	It tells a story about ordinary citizens in Gwangju who fell victims to the violent assaults by the military junta under General Chun Doo-hwan. (poster © CJ Entertainment)

Framing the Gwangju uprising as a violent riot organized by North Korean spies infiltrated into South Korea, the Chun Doo-hwan regime legitimized the indiscriminate killing of ordinary Gwangju citizens, and imprisoned hundreds and thousands of people critical of the government. More than 700 journalists and 86 professors were dismissed from their post, while almost 1,400 students of 65 universities were suspended for political activism (Lee YS, 2013). To muzzle dissenting voices, the Chun regime introduced the "Act for the Protection of Society" which authorized a preventative detention of dissenters for seven to ten years. Between 1980 and 1986, more than 6,000 people were jailed under this Act (Cumings, 2002).

Political Suppression under the Chun regime

The film, "The Attorney", is based on the real story of the "Burim case" (부림사건) in 1981. The Chun regime arrested 22 students, teachers and office workers, who belonged to a book club, and charged them with the violation of the National Security Law. While being illegally detained for more than 2 months, they were tortured and forced to sign a false statement that they were members of a pro-communist organization. Roh Moo-hyun[24], a lawyer, defended the accused people.

Title	The Attorney
Released	2013 (Director: Yang Woo-suk)
Cast	Song Kang-ho, Kim Young-ae, Oh Dal-su, Im Si-wan, Kwak Do-won
Synopsis	The film tells a story about an attorney, fighting for a university student who was framed as a member of a pro-communist organization. (poster © Next Entertainment World)

The film, "National Security 1985" (aka Namyeong-dong 1985, 남영동 1985), is based on the real story of Kim Geun-tae, a pro-democracy activist who later became a member of the Kim Dae-jung administration (1998-2003).

Title	National Security 1985
Released	2012 (Director: Jeong Ji-young)
Cast	Park Won-sang, Lee Geung-young
Synopsis	The film dramatizes the real-life story of Kim Geun-tae, a renowned human rights activist. It focuses on the brutal suppression of pro-democracy movements by the repressive Chun regime in the 1980s. (poster © Megabox/Cinus/Aura Pictures)

---

[24] In 2003, the lawyer Roh Moo-hyun became the 16th president of the ROK.

The Chun regime imprisoned many human rights activists in relation to "Mincheongryeon" (the Association of Youths for Democracy) in 1985, which was framed as a pro-communist organization. Being accused of taking part in the alleged pro-North Korean "Mincheongryeon", Kim was kidnapped by the National Security Planning Agency (NSPA) and was brutally tortured in the NSPA building, located in Namyeongdong.

Keeping all newspapers and radio-television broadcasting operations under the government's tight control, the Chun regime sent many political dissenters along with some homeless people to military bootcamps, known as "Samcheong re-education camps (삼청교육대)" or "Purification Camp." In 1981, some 37,000 people including journalists, students, teachers, labor organizers, and civil servants were sent to the "Purification Camp" in remote mountain areas where they underwent a harsh "re-education" (Cumings, 2002: 26; Oliver, 1993:316).

Collusive Politics under the Chun regime

The TV drama, "Sandglass", dramatizes some major political events under the Chun regime, including the 1980 Gwangju uprising, the Samchung Purification camp, and collusive connections between government officials and corporations.

	Title	Sandglass
	Production	Aired in 1995 (24 episodes)
	Cast	Choi Min-soo, Go Hyun-jung, Park Sang-won
	Synopsis	The film follows the lives of three friends (a prosecutor, a gangster, and a student activist) and their enduring friendship amid the dangerous political situation throughout the late 1970s and 1980s. (poster © SBS)

Aired in 1995, it was the first TV drama that shed light on many controversial issues that had been previously prohibited for open discussion. The drama became highly popular with an average viewership rating of 50% in South Korea. Thanks to the popularity of the drama, all three main characters rose to stardom.

Until the mid-1990s, the production of TV series and films critical of the military dictatorship was not possible due to state censorship. Only with the transition from dictatorship to democracy, the domestic entertainment industry began to show interest in contemporary politics as a source of dramatization. For TV dramas on the contemporary politics of South Korea since 1948, please see the Appendix 1.

* The Emergence of the Pro-democracy Student Movement in the 1980s

In the early 1980s, the expelled students went to factories, slums and rural areas to organize workers, the urban poor, and farmers into trade unions and labor-rights organizations. The pro-democracy movement spread from universities to other sectors of civil society. With the 1985 parliamentary election resulting in the victory of the main opposition party (Minjugdang), the National Assembly passed a series of bills to allow some degree of civil liberties that greatly facilitated the pro-democracy movement. For instance, the police forces withdrew from the campus and, as universities re-gained autonomy, students and faculty members could establish their own representative bodies (Lee N 2002: 151).

With the return of the previously dismissed student activists and professors, anti-government protests on the campus became more frequent and rapidly expanded. Despite the state repression, the pro-democracy movement persisted and by the mid-1980s, it drew hundreds and thousands of students out to open street demonstrations. In the month of May 1985 alone, 30,000 students from 80 universities nationwide held rallies to commemorate the victims of the Gwangju massacre (Lee N 2002: 133).

While hundreds and thousands of student activists and critical intellectuals were imprisoned for demanding civil liberties, many of them experienced ill-treatments including physical and psychological tortures at the hands of the police and state prosecutors. One of the victims fallen to the regime's brutal treatment was Park Jong-chul, a student activist from Seoul National University. In January 1987, he was tortured to death by several police officers, as they forced him to reveal the whereabouts of the leaders of his clandestine student group. The police's torture-killing triggered an avalanche of anti-government street demonstrations that developed into the nation-wide civil disobedience movement calling for a sweeping political reform in June 1987.

At one of the protests, Lee Han-yol, a student protestor at Yonsei University, became fatally injured by fragments of a tear gas canister and died a few days later. The death of Lee Han-yeol came to further strengthen people's resolve to bring down the regime. As more people were hitting the streets, it was reported that about 1.5 million people took part in 247 protests in sixteen cities across the country on June 18, 1987 (Park, SM, 2014). Throughout June, massive demonstrations continued in all major cities and the protestors' chants, "down with the military dictatorship (군사독재타도)", could be heard all over the country.

The Chun administration became divided over the question of how to deal with the political crisis in 1987. Some favored partial political reform, while others supported a military option to quell the protests. The political price would have been too high, if the regime would have put down the protestors by force. With the 1988 Olympic games scheduled to take place in South Korea, the Chun regime was under international spotlight and the June protest movement had already attracted international media attentions. In this context, the Chun regime opted for a political compromise. On June 29, 1987, the government promised a sweeping political reform including constitutional changes to allow a direct presidential election (Park, M 2018). The new constitution introduced a direct presidential election with a 5-year cap on the presidential term and no chance for re-election. With the post-1987 constitution limiting the presidential term to only five years, it also gave considerably more power to the National Assembly and guaranteed civil rights including freedom of speech with some exceptions (Oliver, 1993:323).

Films on the Pro-Democracy Movement of the 1980s

Several movies dealing with the pro-democracy movement of the 1980s have been made in recent years. The film, "1987: When the day comes", is based on the real story of the political events leading to the nation-wide protests in June 1987. The film closely follows the actual events that led

---

to the revelation of the police cover-up of the torture-killing of a university student. It also depicts the June 9 demonstration where Lee Han-yol, a Yonsei university student, was struck by a tear gas canister and died a few days later. Although the film contains some fictional elements, most characters in the film are modelled after real people including Park Jong-chul, Lee Han-yeol, Lee Boo-young and some priests from the Catholic Priests Association for Justice (CPAJ).

	Title	1987: When the Day Comes
	Released	2018 (Director: Jang Joon-hwan)
	Cast	Kim Yoon-seok, Ha Jung-woo, Yu Hae-jin, Kim Tae-ri, Park Hee-soon, Lee Hee-joon, Kang Dong-won
	Synopsis	The film follows the real story about Park Jong-chul's death and the police cover-up. It focuses on the role of some conscientious citizens including a prosecutor, prison guards, journalists, human rights activists, among many others, in bringing the culprits to justice. (poster © CJ Entertainment)

Aside from the movies mentioned above, other films on the same topic are available. For instance, the movie, "The Old Garden", deals with individual traumas of torture and imprisonment that many pro-democracy activists experienced in the 1980s. The movie is based on a novel written by Hwang Sok-yong.

Released in 2017, the film, "Ordinary People (보통사람)" tells a fictional story about the lives of ordinary people in the repressive political system under the Chun Doo-hwan regime. It depicts a series of political events leading to the national protest of 1987. The movie focuses on inner conflicts of ordinary Korean citizens who could not yet join the movement against the dictatorship.

The Roh Tae-Woo Administration (1988-1993)

Notwithstanding some significant political gains, the 1987 protest movement stopped short of a regime change. The Chun administration was followed by the administration led by Chun's right hand man, Roh Tae-woo. Roh was a former military officer who was also deeply involved in the military coup in 1980. The presidential election, held in December 1987, resulted in the victory of the ruling party due to a split of the main opposition party. As the ruling party candidate, Roh Tae-woo, became the main beneficiary from the split votes, he won the election with just 36 percent of the total votes, although the two opposition parties garnered more votes, if counted together (Park, M 2018).

Authoritarianism continued under the Roh Tae-woo administration, albeit to a lesser extent compared to the past. The Roh administration continued to supress the workers' and students' movements for civil rights. The conflict between student-labor activists and the Roh administration came to a head in 1991. The death of a student activist, Gang Gyeong-dae, fueled student demonstrations that coalesced with workers' industrial actions into the massive protest movement. From April and June 1991, South Korea was once again rocked by violent street demonstrations involving clashes between the police and demonstrators. As trade unionists and industrial workers joined the student protest movement, the number of protestors reached over one million in May 1991. The Roh administration was forced to make further political concessions due to the continued pressure from civil society groups.

The Kim Young-sam administration (1993-1997)

Kim Young-sam, leader of one of two main opposition parties, forged a political alliance with Roh's ruling party. With the support of the ruling elite, Kim came to lead the first civilian government after almost three decades of military dictatorship. The Kim administration adopted economic and political policies to liberalize South Korea. As part of his campaign to rectify the historical wrongs, the two former presidents, Chun and Roh, were prosecuted on charges of corruption (bribery and embezzlement) and treason for the 1979 military coup. Although they were sentenced to death in 1996, they were pardoned one year later (Tudor 2012:90).

The Kim Dae-jung Administration (1998-2003)

In 1998, the long-time dissident and leader of the main opposition party, Kim Dae-jung, was inaugurated as President. His government succeeded in overcoming the economic hardship, induced by the International Monetary Fund (IMF) imposed austerity measures on South Korea in the aftermath of the Asian Financial crisis since 1997 (Park, M, 2018). The Kim administration institutionalized workers' industrial action by legalizing trade unions including the Korean Confederation of Trade Unions (KCTU). President Kim Dae-jung carried out progressive political measures that expanded civil rights and curtailed the power of the ANSP (Agency for National Security Planning)[25], the successor to the notorious KCIA (Korea Central Intelligence Agency). As for inter-Korea relations, the Kim Dae-jung government adopted the policy of economic co-operation and cultural exchange (known as the "sunshine policy") towards North Korea. In June 2000, the leaders of the two Koreas met, for the first time, at a summit and agreed to work toward reconciliation and cooperation.

The Roh Moo-hyun Administration (2003-2008)

The Roh Moo-hyun government, inaugurated in 2003, continued to implement and to expand the Sunshine policy, largely shaped by Kim Dae-jung. Following the Sunshine policy, Roh held a second summit with the leader of North Korea, while he further expanded political measures to empower civil society in South Korea. As Snyder put it, "Roh campaigned to revolutionize Korean politics and society by promoting clean politics, fighting corruption, and challenging personal and elite ties as the basis for advancement in Korean society" (Snyder, 2009). Roh was a "political idealist" (Snyder, 2009) who was loved by many Koreans but also equally hated by some, especially in the circle of the elite working for the criminal justice system, the media, and large corporations.

---

[25] As of 1998, with more than 70,000 employees and an annual budget of around $1 billion, the ANSP had hundreds of political dissidents prosecuted (Cumings, 2002:31). Under the Kim administration, the ANSP's budget was cut by 50 percent and the intelligence agency was prohibited to interfere in domestic political affairs (Cumings, 2002:31).

The prosecutors in South Korea enjoy the monopoly of power in terms of criminal investigation and prosecution. Since they completely control the criminal investigation procedure without any judicial supervision, they have an enormous source of information and power over society, as they determine whom to investigate and/or to prosecute (Pyo 2007). The wealthy and the powerful in Korea, therefore, have maintained a cozy relationship with high-rank prosecutors and the elite media.

President Roh tried to reform the nation's criminal justice system but faced an enormous backlash from within, especially among the prosecutors who had enjoyed a cozy relationship with the wealthy elite and corrupt politicians. The main opposition party, supported by the forces with ties to previous dictatorial regimes, tried to bring down the Roh administration by impeaching President Roh Moo-hyeon over a minor violation of election laws. The impeachment attempt failed but the following presidential election resulted in the victory of Lee Myeong-bak, the candidate of the conservative Hannaradang party.

The Nexus of Power: The Prosecutors, Corporations, Politicians, and the Elite Media

The film, "The King", portrays a collusive relationship between prosecutors, politicians and the elite media in South Korea.

	Title	The King
	Released	2017
	Director	Han Jae-rim
		Jo In-sung, Jeong Woo-sung
	Synopsis	The film tells a story about a prosecutor who joins an inner-circle of the powerful prosecutors having close ties with the wealthy people and high-rank government officials. (poster © WooJoo Film/ NEW)

The Lee administration, aided by Korea's National Intelligence Service (NIS) and mainstream media, embarked on carrying out a negative media campaign of spreading fake news about Roh and his family. With the aim to tarnish Roh's reputation based on "clean politics", the Lee government initiated a criminal inquiry into suspicions of bribery surrounding Roh's family. As the political machination against him, his family and his close supporters continued, Roh was subjected to a political witch hunt, daily torment and humiliation, driven by the media closely tied to the powerful prosecutors. Unable to endure the suffering of his family any longer, he put an end to the targeted political inquiry by committing suicide.

As later revealed, Roh's prosecution for corruption was politically orchestrated by the conservative Lee administration. Only after the inauguration of the Moon Jae-in administration in 2017, an investigation into his death found that the Lee administration and the NIS were directly responsible for the political machinations and the negative media campaign.

Roh Moo-hyun

Many Koreans regard Roh Moo-hyun as a progressive President who fell victim to the political machination engineered by the Lee administration, the NIS, and the elite media. In recent years, a few documentary films have been made to remember the progressive role that the former President Roh had played in bolstering civil rights. "Our President" and "Roh Moo-hyun and the fools" are classic documentary films that strictly follow a biographical story of President Roh.

Title	Our President (aka 노무현 입니다)
Released	2017
Director	Lee Chang-jae/Yang Hee
Synopsis	This documentary film follows the political career of President Roh from his rise to power to his death. (poster © 영화사풀)

The Lee Myung-bak Administration (2008-2013)

In 2008, the governmental power shifted to the conservative Grand National Party (Hannaradang 한나라당, 2008-2012) that rooted in the political forces closely tied to the previous authoritarian regimes. The candidate of the conservative Grand National Party, Lee Myung-bak, was elected to president. Lee introduced many controversial economic policies such as several hydro-dam projects, the privatization of health insurance and public enterprises (water and electricity) as well as a beef import deal with the US.

Lee's authoritarian decision to import US beef without proper public consultation angered the public. Many Koreans were deeply concerned about the inadequate safety measures to screen out the beef infected with mad cow disease. In this context, many individual citizens and civic groups organized candlelight vigils to repeal the beef agreement. On 10 June 2008, more than one million people attended the rally to denounce the US beef deal. Facing the strong domestic opposition, the Lee administration amended the beef importation agreement (Park, M 2018).

Meantime, President Lee brought back some authoritarian measures to muzzle critics. Making undemocratic changes to the educational system and mass media, the Lee administration rolled back some polices of the previous liberal administrations. The Lee government ordered the National Intelligence Service (NIS) to compile a blacklist of media personnel and cultural figures who criticized Lee's policies. The NIS barred the blacklisted people from appearing on public broadcasters and they were dismissed from important management positions (Park M, 2018).

The Park Geun-hye Administration (2013-2017)

Despite the unpopularity of the Lee administration, the conservative ruling party secured power once again with the election of Park Geun-hye, the oldest daughter of Park Chung-hee, the former military dictator. The Park Geun-hye administration signed controversial treaties with Japan concerning the "Comfort women" issue and the Korea-Japan bilateral agreement on military information sharing that angered many Koreans. The sinking of the Sewol ferry that took away hundreds of student passengers in 2014 made many Koreans deeply unhappy with the conduct of the Park administration. The government's incompetent rescue measures during the last hours of the

Sewol ferry came under heavy fire from the public. As in the case with the Lee administration, President Park responded to her critics with authoritarian measures such as penalizing blacklisted dissenters (Park M, 2018).

A Film on the Sewol Ferry Tragedy

While several documentary films on the Sewol Ferry tragedy exist, not many commercial films have been made so far to shed light on the Korean society gripped with the Sewol Ferry tragedy of 2014. The films, "Birthday" and "Bad Police", are the two most recent films touching on the issue.

	Title	Birthday
	Released	2019 (Director: Lee Jong-un)
	Cast	Jeon Do-yeon, Sol Kyung-gu
	Synopsis	This is the first commercial film that used the tragic sinking of Sewol Ferry as its historical background. The film portrays the life of a couple who lost their son to the Sewol Ferry tragedy. (Poster © Nowfilm/ Next Entertainment)

In 2016, a corruption scandal involving President Park surfaced. It was revealed that President Park and her friend, Choi Soon-Sil, abused public funds of various governmental bodies including the National Intelligence Agency (NIA). They also took briberies from Korea's big conglomerates (chaebols). They established two non-profit organizations (the Mir and K Sport Foundations) as conduits for financial extortion and money laundering. The two foundations received millions of dollars from major chaebols including Samsung, Hyundai, SK, and Lotte (Park, M 2018).

Outraged at the corruption in the government, millions of citizens took to the streets to demand the resignation of Park Geun-hye. When Park refused to take responsibility for her wrong-doings, citizens' demand changed from her voluntary resignation to an impeachment. An overwhelming majority, almost 80% of the Korean population, demanded that the National Assembly should impeach her. On December 3, 2016, a record number of people, 2.32 million, attended the nation-wide vigil to demand Park's impeachment. Due to the enormous pressure from the public, the National Assembly eventually impeached Park Geun-hye in late 2016. The parliamentary decision of Park's impeachment was validated by the Constitutional Court in early 2017 (Park M 2018). This processes starting from the candlelight protest in 2016 to the peaceful regime change in 2017 are referred to the Candlelight Revolution (촛불혁명) (Park M, 2018).

The Candlelight Revolution

The film, "Gwanghwa: History Making with Candlelight (광화: 촛불로 역사를 피우다) is the first documentary film dealing with the Candlelight Revolution that brought down the Park Geun-hye government in 2016.

	Title	Gwanghwa: History Making with Candlelight
	Released	2019 (Cinemadal production)
	Director	Kim Cheol-min et.al.
	Synopsis	This documentary film details the candlelight vigils and the political processes leading to the downfall of the Park administration. (Poster © Cinemadal).

The Moon Jae-in Administration (2017- present)

In May 2017, Moon Jae-in, the candidate of the main opposition Democratic Party, was elected to presidential office. He promised to complete the Candlelight Revolution by bringing wrongdoers to justice and to restore democracy. President Moon is no stranger to the pro-democracy movement, as he himself was a student activist and a human rights lawyer, who was imprisoned for his opposition to the military dictatorship in the 1970s.

Appendix 1 List of Historical K-dramas and films

Period	K-dramas and Films
Post-Gojoseon	Jumong (주몽), Jamyeong-go (자명고)
Silla (57 BC-668AD)	Hwarang (화랑), Queen Seondeok (선덕여왕), Hwangsanbeol (황산벌), Pyeongyangsung (평양성)
Goguryeo (37 BC-668 AD)	Jumong (주몽), The Kingdom of the Wind (바람의 나라), Jamyeong-go (자명고), The Legend (태왕사신기), King Gwanggaeto the Great (광개토태왕), The Great Hero (Yeon Gaesomun 연개소문), Sword and Flower (칼과꽃). Dae Jo-young (대조영).
Baekje (18 BC -660 AD)	King Geunchogo (근초고왕), The King's Daughter, Soo Baek-hyang (왕의딸 백수향), Ballade of Seo Dong (서동요), Gyebaek: The Great King's Dream (계백), Thousand Years of Love (천년지애)
Kaya (42-532 AD)	Kim Soo-ro (김수로)
Unified Silla (668-935)	King's Dream (대왕의 꿈), Emperor of the Sea (해신), Emperor Wang Gun, Taejo Wang Gun (태조왕건), The Legend of Evil Lake (천년호)
Balhae (698-926)	Dae Jo-yeong (대조영), Shadowless Sword (무영검)
Goryeo (918-1392)	Moon lovers: Scarlet Heart Ryeo, Bi Chun Mu (비천무), Warrior (무사), Taejo Wang Gun (태조 왕건), Shine or go crazy (빛나거나 미치거나), Dawn of the Empire (제국의 아침), The Age of Warrior (무인시대), God of War (무신), The Iron Empress (천추태후), Faith (신의), Tears of the Dragon (용의눈물), The King Loves (왕은 사랑한다), Empress Ki (기황후), The Great Seer (대풍수), Shin Don (신돈), Jeong Do-jeon (정도전), Six Flying Dragons (육룡이 나르샤)
Joseon Kingdom	**K-dramas and Films**
The First King, Taejo 태조 (r. 1392-1398)	Six Flying Dragons (육룡이 나르샤), Tears of the Dragon (용의눈물)

The Second King, Jeongjong (정종 r. 1399-1400)	Tears of the Dragon (용의눈물)
The Third King, Taejong (태종 r.1400-1418)	Empire of Lust (순수의 시대), The Face Reader (관상), Tears of the Dragon (용의눈물)
The Fourth King, Sejong (세종 r. 1418-1450)	Jan Yeong-sil (장영실), King Sejong the Great (대왕세종), Tree with Deep Roots (뿌리깊은 나무)
The Fifth King, Munjong (문종 r. 1450-1452)	Queen Insoo (인수대비)
The Sixth King, Danjong (단종 r. 1452-1455)	King and Queen (왕과비)
The 7th King, Sejo (세조 r.1455-1468)	Han Myung Hoe (한명회) , The Princess' Man (공주의 남자)
The 9th King, Seongjong 성종 (r.1469-1494)	Hong Gildong (홍길동), Fast Sword Hong Gildong (쾌도 홍길동)
The 10th King, Yeonsangun 연산군 (r.1494-1506)	The King and I (왕과나), Jang Nok Soo (장녹수), Jeon Woo Chi (전우치), Seven Day Queen (7일의 왕비)
The 11th King, Joongjong 중종 (r.1506-1544)	Jewel in the Palace (대장금), Ladies of the Palace (여인천하) , Im Kkeok Jung (임꺽정), Hwang Jin-yi (황진이), Saimdang, Lights' Diary (사임당, 빛의 일기)
The 12th King, Injong 인종 (r. 1544-1545)	Rebel: Thief who stole the people (역적: 백성을 훔친 도둑)
The 14th King, Seonjo 선조 (r. 1567-1608) * Japanese Invasion (1592-8)	Immortal Admiral Lee Soon-sin (불멸의 이순신), The Legendary doctor-Heo Jun (허준) , Guam Heo Jun (구암허준), The King's Face (왕의 얼굴), The King's Woman (왕의 여자), Book of the House of Gu (구가의 서), The Jingbirok: A Memoir of Imjin War (징비록), The Imjin War 1592 (임진왜란 1592), The Admiral: Roaring Currents (명량), Blades of Blood (aka Like the Moon Escaping from the Clouds 구르믈 버서난 달처럼), The Legend of the Blue Sea (푸른바다의 전설)
The 15th King, Kwanghaegun 광해군 (r. 1608-1623)	The Return of Iljimae (돌아온 일지매), Iljimae (일지매), West Palace (서궁)
The 16th King, Injo (인조 r. 1623-1649)	Hwajung (화정), The Three Musketeers (삼총사), Mighty Chil-woo (최강 칠우), Cruel Palace: War of Flowers (궁중잔혹사:

* The Manchu Invasions (1627, &1636-1637)	꽃의 전쟁), Horse Doctor (마의), The Reputable Family (명가), Bow: the Ultimate Weapon (Movie), The Slave Hunters (추노)
The 19th King, Sookjong (숙종 r. 1674-1720)	Scholar Who Walks the Night (밤을걷는 선비), Jang Hee-bin (장희빈), Jang Ok-Jung, Living by Love (장옥정 사랑에 살다), Dong Yi (동이), Jang Gil-san (장길산), Damo (다모)
The 21st King, Yeongjo (영조 r. 1724-1776)	Inspector Park Moon-soo (어사 박문수), Jackpot (대박), Ruler: Master of the Mask (군주: 가면의 주인), The Road of the Great King (대왕의 길), The Throne (or Sado 사도)
The 22nd King, Jeongjo (정조 r. 1776-1800)	Painter of the Wind (바람의 화원), Lee San, Wind of the Palace (이산), Merchant Kim Man-deok (거상 김만덕), Secret Door (비밀의 문: 의궤 살인사건), Sangdo (상도), Jeong Yak-yong (조선추리활극 정약용), Wangdo (왕도), Hong Gook-yeong (홍국영), Sungkyungwan Scandal (성균관 스캔들), Yeokrin (역린), Warrior Baek Dong-soo (무사 백동수)
The 25th King, Cheoljong (철종 r. 1849-1864)	Kundo: Age of the Rampant (군도)
King, Gojong (고종 r. 1864-1907) King, Sunjong (순종 r. 1907-1910)	Taeyangin Lee Je-ma (태양인 이제마), The Merchant: Gaekju (장사의 신), Gunman in Joseon (조선총잡이), Je Jung Won (제중원), Byeolsungeom (조선과학 수사대 별순검), Mr. Sunshine, The Sword with No Name, The Righteous Army: The Age of Heroes (의군: 푸른 영웅의 시대), Myeongsung-hwanghoo (명성황후), Daewongun (대원군), The Splendid Dawn (찬란한 여명), The Land (토지), Gabi (가비), Mung Bean Flower (녹두꽃)
Colonial Period (1910-1945)	**K-dramas and Films**
Japanese Occupation (1910-1945)	Assassination (암살), Prince Deokhye (덕혜옹주), Thomas An Joong-geun (도마 안중근), Spirits coming (귀향), The Battleship Island (군함도), Dong-ju (동주), The Age of Shadow (밀정), Anarchist from colony (Park Yeol), Bridal Mask (각시탈), Praise of Death (사의찬미), Capital Scandal, Anarchist (아나키스트), Freedom Fighter, Lee Hoe-young (자유인 이회영), Different Dreams (이몽), Inspiring Generation (감격시대), YMCA

Baseball Team, The Good, the Bad, the Weird (좋은 놈, 나쁜 놈, 이상한 놈), The Last Comfort Women (마지막 위안부), A Resistance: The Story of Yoo Gwan-sun (항거: 유관순 이야기), Tuning Fork (소리굽쇠), The Eyes of Dawn (여명의 눈), Journal of Baekbeom (백범일지), War and Peace (전쟁과 사랑), Mimang (미망), The Righteous Army: The Age of Heroes (의군: 푸른 영웅의 시대),

1945-2017	K-dramas and Films
American Military Government (1945-1948) & The Republic of Korea (1948)	The Eyes of Dawn (여명의 눈), Taebaek Mountains (태백산맥), Camellia (동백), The Age of Heroes (영웅시대), Land (땅), Seoul 1945 (서울 1945), Haewon (해원)
The Korean War (1950-1953)	Tae Geuk Gi (태극기 휘날리며), The Front Line (고지전), Into the Fire (포화속으로)
Inter-Korea Relations (1954-Present)	Silmido (실미도), Shiri (쉬리), Joint Security Area (공동경비구역 JSA), The Berlin File (베를린파일), IRIS (아이리스), The King 2 Hearts (더킹투하츠), Blood Brother (의형제), Steel Rain (강철비), Secretly Greatly (은밀하게 위대하게), Confidential Assignment (공조), Korea as One (코리아), City Hunter (시티헌터)
Rhee Seung-man Administration (1948-1960)	The President's Barber (효자동이발사), Low Life (하류인생), Going Well (잘 돼갑니다). My Sister's March (누나의 3월), The First Republic (제 1 공화국), The Second Republic (제 2 공화국)
Park Chung-hee Administration (1961-1979)	The Aesthetics of Yushin (유신의 미학), The Third Republic (제 3 공화국), The Fourth Republic (제 4 공화국), The Korea Gate (코리아게이트), A Single Spark (아름다운 청년 전태일), The Era of Three Kims (삼김시대), Ode to My Father (국제시장)
Chun Doo-hwan Administration (1980-1987)	Sandglass (유리시계), Splendid Holiday, 1987: When the Day Comes (1987: 그날이 오면), Ordinary People (보통사람), The Fifth Republic (제 5 공화국), Butterfly (나비), The President's Last Bang (그때

188

	그사람들), Peppermint Candy (박하사탕), A Petal (꽃잎), National Security 1985 (남영동), Taxi Driver (택시운전사), The Attorney (변호인), The Old Garden (오래된 정원)
Post-1987 Administrations	1991 Spring (1991 봄), 26 Years (26 년), Our President (노무현입니다), Roh Moo-hyun and the Fools (노무현과 바보들), Birthday (생일), Bad Cop (악질경찰), Gwanghwa (광화: 촛불로 역사를 피우다)

Reference

Anderson, Benedict (1991) *Imagined Communities: Reflections on the Origin and Spread of Nationalism.* Verso.

Asian Women's Fund (no date) "The Life in Comfort Stations". The Comfort Women Issue and Asian Women's Fund. Digital Museum. http://www.awf.or.jp/e1/facts-12.html

Blakenmore, Erin (2018) "How Japan Took Control of Korea". https://www.history.com/news/japan-colonization-korea

Chung, Annika (2018) *All About K-pop. Inside Stories behind K-pop's Rise to Global Fandom.* Coal Harbour Publishing

Cumings, Bruce (2002) "Civil Society in West and East" In: Armstrong, Charles K. (ed) *Korean Society: civil society, democracy, and the state.* Routledge

Han, Suzanne Crowder (1995) *Notes on Things Korean.* Hollym

Heo Wan (2018) "제주 4.3 사건'이 아직 낯선 당신이 알아야 할 7 가지.비극은 끝났지만, 끝나지 않았다." Huffington Post. 2018 년 4 월 3 일 by 허 완

Joe, Wannne J (2000) *A Cultural History of Modern Korea: A History of Korean Civilization.* (한국 근대문화사) Authored by Cho Wan-je(조 완제) Hollym.

Kim, Sam-ung (2019b) *항일의 불꽃. 의열단.* 김삼웅 지음.두레출판사.

Kim, Ho-gyung (12 August 2017) "군함도, 영화와 실제 사이". Newsis.

Kim, Min-cheol et. al (2018) *군함도. 끝나지않은 전쟁.* 민족문제연구소 기획. 김민철, 김승은 외 지음. 생각정원.

Kim, Sam-ung (2019a) *3.1 혁명과 임시정부.* 김삼웅 지음. 두레 출판사.

Lee Ki-baik (1984) *A New History of Korea.* Translated by Edward W. Wagner. Harvard University Press.

Lee, Hyeon-Ee (1995) "105 인 사건". *The Encyclopedia of Korean Culture* 한국민족문화대백과사전

Lee, Namhee (2002) "The South Korean student movement: Undongkwon as a counterpublic sphere" In: Armstrong, Charles K. (ed) *Korean Society: civil society, democracy, and the state*. Routledge

Macdonald, Donald Stone (1996) *The Koreans. Contemporary Politics and Society*. 3rd edition. Westview Press.

New World Encyclopedia. (28 March 2017) Gojoseon.

Oliver, Robert T. (1993) *A History of the Korean People in Modern Times. 1800 to the Present*. University of Delaware Press: Newark & Associated University Presses: London and Toronto.

Park, Mi (2018) *South Korea's Candlelight Revolution. The Power of Plaza Democracy*. Coal Harbour Publishing.

Park, Mi (2018) The *IMF* and *WTO*: *How does geopolitics influence global finance and international trade?* Cola Harbour Publishing

Pratt, Keith and Richard Rutt (1999) *Korea. A Historical and Cultural Dictionary*. Curzon.

Pyo, Changwon (2007) Prosecutor, Police and Criminal Investigation in Korea: A Critical Review. *Journal of Korean Law,* Vol. 6, No. 2, 2007

Renan, Ernest (1882) *What is a Nation?* Translated and edited by M. F. N. Giglioli. Columbia University Press

Reuters (30 October 2018) "South Korea court orders Japan firm to compensate wartime forced laborers"

Richards, Kay (2004) Yoon Dong-ju's poem, "One Night I Count the Stars." In McCann (Ed), *The Columbian Anthology of Modern Korean Poetry*.

SBS News (15 August 2009) "윤동주, 일제 생체실험에 희생" 죽음의 미스터리.

Seth, Michael J. (2006) *A Concise History of Korea. From the Neolithic Period through the Nineteenth Century*. Rowman & Littlefield Publishers

Shams, Shamil (2019) "The Jallianwala massacre – when British troops killed hundreds of unarmed Indians". *Deutsche Welle*. 13 April 2019.

Shin, Chae-ho (2014) 조 완제 *조선상고사. 국사교과서가 가르쳐주지 않은 우리역사.* 단재 신채호 지음. 김 종성 옮김. 역사의 아침.

Sisa Journal (1 September 2018) "인간 병기 위해 지옥 훈련 '죽음의 땅". 시사저널

The Diplomat (21 July 2015) "Japanese Company Apologizes for Forced Labor During World War II". By Shannon Tiezzi

The Hankyoreh (1 November 2017)108년 전 오늘, 창경궁은 동물원이 됐다

The Korea Times (24 February 2010) "Coal Miners Sent to Germany: Forgotten Chapter of Koreas Nation Building."

The Korea Times (8 November 2009) "Park Chung-hee Leads List of Collaborators with Japan".

Tudor, Daniel (2012) *Korea. The Impossible Country*. Tuttle Publishing.

Yonhap News (26 February 2019) "3 · 1 운동.임정 百주년 (35) 밀정 피살 항일무장투쟁가 박용만"

Photo Credits

Coal Harbour Book Series on Korea

South Korea's Candlelight Revolution. The Power of Plaza Democracy (by Mi Park)

All about K-pop. Inside Stories behind K-pop's Rise to Global Fandom (by A. Chung)

Learn Korean Language with K-pop Song Lyrics! Vol 1, 2, & 3 (by A. Chung)

Beautiful Sceneries from Seoul to Jejudo (by Chrystal Lee)

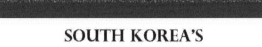

SOUTH KOREA'S
CANDLELIGHT REVOLUTION

THE POWER OF PLAZA DEMOCRACY

MI PARK
COAL HARBOUR PUBLISHING

Between October 2016 and April 2017, more than 17 million South Koreans took to the streets to demand the resignation of President Park Geun-hye over a corruption scandal involving the Park administration. Without a single arrest or casualty, the 2016-2017 candlelight protests paved the way for a peaceful regime change in South Korea. In stark contrast to Korea's past when pro-democracy protests had been crushed by armed forces, the Korean people have ensured a peaceful and orderly transition of power. Exploring socio-political factors that contributed to the success of the Candlelight Revolution, this book sheds light on Korea's creative protest culture and the power of plaza democracy.

Made in United States
Orlando, FL
28 January 2022